Barbara Ellis, Editor

Frances Tenenbaum, Series Editor

HOUGHTON MIFFLIN COMPANY

Boston • New York 1997

Plants for Problem Places

LINDA YANG

How to turn any difficult site into
a beautiful easy-care garden

Copyright © 1997 by Houghton Mifflin Company
Text copyright © 1997 by Linda Yang

For information about permission to reproduce selections from this book,
write to Permissions, Houghton Mifflin Company, 215 Park Avenue South,
New York, New York 10003.

For information about this and other Houghton Mifflin trade
and reference books and multimedia products, visit The Bookstore at
Houghton Mifflin on the World Wide Web at http://www.hmco.com/trade/.

Taylor's Guide is a registered trademark of Houghton Mifflin Company.

Library of Congress Cataloging-in-Publication Data

Yang, Linda
Plants for Problem places : dependable species for difficult garden spots / Linda Yang.
    p. cm. — (Taylor's weekend gardening guides ; 10)
    Includes index.
    ISBN 0-395-82762-0
    1. Plants, Ornamental. 2. Plants, Ornamental — Selection. 3. Landscape gardening.
    I. Title. II. Series.
    SB407.Y25 1997
    635.9—dc21   97-22929

Printed in the United States of America.

WCT 10 9 8 7 6 5 4 3 2 1

Book design by Deborah Fillion
Cover photograph © by Ken Druse

Contents

R are is the garden with no problem place. As a bonafide member of the dirty-fingernail crowd, I admit to dreaming of an idyllic retreat where reality does not intrude. For sooner or later, anyone who tills the soil must confront the rude spots in the landscape. Too many gardeners exhaust themselves trying to use plants that don't like their conditions or trying to redo conditions to suit their plants. Both are a waste of time. And both can be destructive — to the garden as well as the gardener, who is sure to conclude that planting is only fraught with frustration.

But there's no need for despair. There *is* a "good" plant for every "problem" place, a dependable species for every difficult garden spot. It's just a matter of making a match. And that's what this book is about. Here, several hundred plants are organized according to their ability to serve. These groupings are planned to help both the novice gardener facing a first spring, and the experienced gardener facing a simmering embarrassment.

As a friend once said — and I think it's so — in making a garden we improve reality.

---

*This medley of fillers and covers among the rocks includes lavender-flowered Chinese astilbe (*Astilbe chinensis *'Pumila') and evergreen periwinkle (*Vinca minor*).*

Chapter 1:
Coverups for Bare Walls, Fences, and Eyesores

We were barely ensconced in our new townhouse when my son lodged his first complaint. "I hate that wall. And I don't want to see it!" He was wailing about a neighbor's four-story brick facade. In less than five years his wish was granted. Our side of the structure had disappeared beneath an undulating green curtain of Boston ivy.

It's not for nothing vines have been called nature's drapery. And what nicer way to clothe a naked wall, fence, or trellis or conceal an immovable eyesore? My vine grew at incredible speed — thanks to unrelenting doses of the maximum allowable fertilizer. Yet even left to their own devices, as Donald Wyman, the eminent horticulturist once told me, vines are rapid growers that easily outstrip all other woody plants.

But not all vines ascend the same way. So to be sure that yours succeeds in getting up in the world — and providing the blanket you need — match the plant with the surface to be garbed.

The trumpet-shaped blooms of honeysuckle (Lonicera heckrottii) *brighten a lattice-covered building. White feverfew enhances its base.*

FOR BROAD, FLAT SURFACES

For a broad, flat area, the vine to use is one that clings either by aerial rootlets or holdfasts along its stem, or by tiny suction-cup-like discs. These natural fasteners are ideal for blanketing walls or structures of stone, brick, or concrete.

Unfortunately, vines that ascend this way have been falsely accused of damaging their supports, when in fact they do no harm; these aerial rootlets are primarily climbing mechanisms and not roots looking for moisture or nutrients. Climbing vines have even been shown to have a beneficial effect on homes by keeping walls cooler in summer and warmer in winter, thus reducing the thermal tensions that inspire masonry cracks. Stems, however, may enter loose joints and aggravate existing faults. Climbing vines should not be used on wood structures or those that need regular refinishing.

■ *Campis radicans* / Trumpet Vine

Hardy deciduous vine

Zone 5

Sun or part shade

The first time I saw this vine I was sure it had escaped from the Caribbean, so tropical are the funnel-shaped summer flowers that hummingbirds adore. But it's a tough native North American. It's also a vigorous grower that becomes top-heavy with age, so have your pruners ready. If the easily rooting suckers spread where you don't want them, sever with a sharp spade. 'Flava' blooms in yellow, 'Madame Galen' has apricot flowers, and 'Crimson Trumpet' is true to its name. By autumn, the floral remains are cigar-shaped seed capsules.

■ *Hedera helix* / English Ivy

Hardy evergreen vine

Zones vary

Sun and part or full shade

A symbol of intellectual achievement in ancient Rome, English ivy was carried to America by the colonists. Now happily at home here — even invasive in some areas — it flourishes undeterred by poor soil, drought, or shade. The many cultivars include delightfully variegated and ruffled forms, but not all are reliably hardy in frosty climes. If you see one you can't resist, do experiment. But if frost survival is essential, beg a seedling from a neighbor's successful plant. 'Baltica', '238th Street', 'Pittsburgh', and 'Thorndale' have solid reputations for hardiness.

■ *Hydrangea petiolaris* / **Climbing Hydrangea**

Hardy deciduous vine

Zone 5

Sun or part shade

A 19th-century immigrant from the Orient, this handsome climber is finally receiving its just due. A slow starter whose lacy, flat-topped, white June flowers may not appear for several years, its shiny oval leaves more than compensate for the wait. I helped my new plant gain a quick foothold by taping its stems to its wall support with adhesive. Autumn brings golden foliage, and the winter is a tangle of rough auburn stems. A cousin with similar attributes but later flowers is *Schizophragma integrifolium*.

■ *Parthenocissus tricuspidata* / **Boston Ivy**

Hardy deciduous vine

Zone 5

Sun and part or full shade

I laughed when a friend dubbed this the "Ivy-league ivy," but it certainly is a ubiquitous presence around colleges. An easily grown plant, quickly soaring to astonishing heights, it's not a Bostonian at all, but a native of China and Japan. The three-lobed leaves resemble those of maples but the shape varies as the plant matures. Autumn brings crimson leaves and blue-black berries that birds adore.

> **TIPS FOR SUCCESS**
>
> **KNOW YOUR FERTILIZER**
>
> Prominently listed on all fertilizer packages are three hyphenated numbers (for example, 5-10-5). These stand for the percentages of nitrogen (N), phosphoric acid (P), and potassium or potash (K), in just that order. Nitrogen promotes good leaf growth; phosphorus encourages the maturity that leads to flowering and fruiting; and potassium promotes hardiness, disease resistance, and good root development. Plants also need minute quantities of other nutrients, called trace elements, and if these are present, they too will be listed on the label.

FOR OPEN FENCES OR LATTICEWORK

If it's not a solid surface you need to blanket, a twining vine is the plant to grow. In frosty climes, only a hardy vine gives permanent cover. But annuals and tender perennial vines are superb summer quickies.

For easy matchmaking between surface and plant, the twining types can be divided into two basic groups. One (like wisteria) climbs by wrapping or twining its entire stem around the support and is useful for draping heavy posts, thick railings, or arbors. This type will also overwhelm a telephone pole, water tower, or TV cable — which may be good for you, but the utility company won't be thrilled. Just keep these hardy wrappers from hugging your favorite tree: eventually it will be strangled as the vine's stem thickens.

The other type (like clematis) climbs by using tendrils — or sometimes, more correctly, petioles — which are tiny appendages along the stem that look like delicate curled hairs. These tough ringlets never fail to astonish in their ability to secure a hold. As they race skyward, these vines will quickly cover a narrow support, thin trellis, wire mesh, or string.

Both types of twiners are capable of transforming even the most hideous chain-link fence into a thing of beauty — well, almost.

The Gardener's Friend

I say it's the earthworm — not the dog — that's really Man's Best Friend. It's not for nothing they're known as "nature's plow," burrowing to great depths, loosening the soil, and improving its structure so that air and water can penetrate. Organic matter passes through their bodies, and their dark castings are superb sources of nutrients. Earthworms live only in humusy, moist soils, and when conditions suit them, they'll appear.

With sun and sturdy support, climbing roses will beautify any surface.

- *Aristolochia durior* / Dutchman's-pipe

Hardy deciduous twiner

Zone 4

Sun or part shade

If heavy Victorian drapery appeals, this is the vine for you, with its densely packed, kidney-shaped, monster-sized foliage. And I do mean monster: a single leaf may grow to nearly 14 inches. In June, tucked among the leaves are 1½-inch tubular, brownish purple flowers with a yellow throat. These tiny U-shaped blooms, which give the vine its common name, do resemble small pipes or little saxophones.

- *Clematis* spp. / Clematis

Hardy deciduous tendrils

Zones vary

Sun or part shade

Those in the know, know to say KLEMatis. But even those who don't will be smitten by the beauty of the 300 or so species and innumerable hybrids. Less fussy than once believed, clematis vines are happiest with rich, well-drained soil and a mulch to keep their roots cool. The range of flower size, shape, color, and season of bloom is extraordinary and, as I have discovered, addiction to these plants is a real danger. Some notables include *C. montana* 'Rubens' (pale pink late-spring flowers), 'Mrs. Cholmondeley' (lavender blue in summer), 'Comtesse de Bouchaud' (pale pink in summer), *C. jackmanii* 'Superba' (purple, summer), *C. viticella* 'Etoile Violette' (purple in summer), and the sweet autumn clematis *C. maximowicziana* (white in autumn). Long-lasting, prominent feathery seed-pods follow the blooms.

- *Ipomoea alba* / **Moonflower** and *Ipomoea purpurea* / **Morning Glory**

Annual twiners

Sun or light shade

It's only natural to list these cousins together. Morning glory welcomes the summer day with many vase-shaped flowers from hybrids such as 'Heavenly Blue'

(blue) and 'Scarlett O'Hara' (crimson). Moonflower's intensely fragrant evening blooms open around martini time as my husband, drink in hand in the garden at 5 P.M., has observed. And martini glasses are just what these 6-inch luminescent white flowers look like.

■ *Lonicera* spp. / Honeysuckle *(See photo on page 2.)*
Hardy deciduous or semievergreen twiner
Zones vary
Sun or part shade
The many honeysuckle vines, with their clusters of tubular flowers, make quick, colorful covers. And while many tolerate more shade than they're given credit for, good sun definitely inspires better flowers. If the scarlet red flowers of *L. sempervirens* 'Magnifica' seem too strong, try *L. s.* 'Sulphurea', whose flowers are yellow. The Goldflame honeysuckle *(L. heckrottii)* has fragrant summer-long flowers, carmine outside and gold inside. Hall's honeysuckle *(L. japonica* 'Halliana') is deliciously fragrant, but this tough plant is a rapid grower that can be dangerously rampant, especially if you're near open woodlands. It has ivory-colored flowers and nearly evergreen leaves at least as far north as Boston.

■ *Rosa* spp. / Climbing Roses
Hardy deciduous shrub
Zones vary
Sun or light shade
To begin with, roses don't "climb." They lean — beautifully. And one day someone will correct this misnomer. Until then, take advantage of their long shoots (or canes) and color a needy trellis, post, or fence. Roses named as "climbers" often bloom intermittently through the summer, while the "ramblers" bloom only once, sometimes for weeks. Both tend to bloom more freely when their canes are trained horizontally. Typically, the more sun, the more flowers, although in my partly shaded garden 'Blaze' has a good early-summer show with sporadic repeating. Other repeaters are 'Don Juan' (dark red) and 'Golden Showers' (yellow).

ADDITIONAL COVERUPS FOR OPEN FENCES OR LATTICEWORK

- *Actinida polygama* / Kiwi

Hardy deciduous twiner

Zone 5

Sun or part shade

By autumn, the white flowers of the kiwi have produced (on female plants only) delicious edible fruit.

A clipped screen of firethorn (Pyracantha) beautifies a stockade fence. At the base, red and white caladium add a splash of summer color.

- *Cobaea scandens* / Cup and Saucer Vine

Tender tendrils

Sun or part shade

The small, pale green to purple summer flowers do vaguely resemble tiny cups and saucers.

- *Dolichos lablab* / Hyacinth Bean

Annual twiner

Sun or light shade

This quick grower is easily grown from seed and its purple-lavender summer flowers are followed by stunning purple seedpods.

- *Lagenaria siceraria* / Bottle Gourd

Annual tendrils

Sun

The white summer flowers are followed by fruit that are indeed shaped like a bottle.

- *Polygonum aubertii* / Silverlace Vine or Fleece Vine

Hardy deciduous twiner

Zone 5

Sun and part or full shade

A fleecy profusion of late-summer lacy-looking white flowers gives this vine its two common names.

- *Wisteria* spp. / Wisteria

Hardy deciduous twiner

Zones vary

Sun or part shade

Sometimes, this tough, quick grower takes years before bearing its white or lilac purple early-summer flowers. A strong support is needed for its heavy stems.

A simple wood fence is embellished with an elegant espaliered pear.

Flat and Fancy: the Espalier

No collection of wall covers would be complete without another kind of plant that, unlike vines, does not cling so much as lean. These are the espaliers — shrubs and small trees that have been coerced into growing flattened in a single plane. Espaliers may be set snug against a wall, fence, or lattice, or stood as free-standing dividers, a trait that makes them especially useful where space is limited.

Dating at least from ancient Rome, espaliers have traditionally been fruiting species, which professionals took pains, and years, to create. The goal was maximum yield in minimum space. The word comes from the French — *épaule* or shoulder — and the Italian, *spella,* meaning a kind of support. It is now used to refer not only to the trained plant itself but to the process of training.

The basic espalier shape is the cordon — French for cord or rope — which in espalier-speak means a plant growing in a single, slender line. A cordon can be trained in either a vertical, horizontal, or diagonal direction, or bent into a candelabra or double U. A series of overlapping diagonal cordons forms the Belgium fence, a luxurious and extremely decorative diamond grid.

Once used only for fruiting plants, nurseries now offer many purely ornamental and modestly priced trained species all ready to be packed in a car, toted home, and plopped in wherever needed. You can also make your own espalier simply by choosing a plant with flexible limbs and a tolerance for pruning. Use a lattice or wire form as a guide, and bend the limbs to conform to the shape. Tie the branches with rubber bands or twist-ties, secure new shoots as they emerge, and regularly snip off stragglers to keep the outline clean.

Here are several hardy woody plants amenable to being espaliered.

■ *Azalea* spp. / **Azalea**
Evergreen
Zones vary
Sun and part or full shade
White, red, or pink spring flowers.

■ *Cotoneaster divaricatus* / **Cotoneaster**
Deciduous
Zone 5
Sun or part shade
Pale pink early-summer flowers, red autumn berries.

■ *Cydonia oblonga* / **Quince**
Deciduous
Zone 6
Sun or light shade
White or pink early-summer flowers and golden yellow fruit.

■ *Forsythia* spp. / **Forsythia**
Deciduous
Zones vary
Sun or part shade
Yellow spring flowers.

A fan-shaped crab apple adds a graceful note to an austere masonry wall.

- *Ilex crenata* / **Japanese Holly**

Evergreen

Sun or part shade

White spring flowers.

- *Malus* spp. / **Crab Apple**

Deciduous

Zones vary

Sun and part or full shade

White, red, or pink spring flowers, red-orange autumn foliage, and red or orange fruit.

Autumn brings glowing orange fruit to a firethorn (Pyracantha) *secured to a wood frame.*

■ *Pyracantha* spp. / **Firethorn**
Evergreen or semievergreen
Zones vary
Sun or part shade
White early-summer flowers and orange autumn fruit.

■ *Taxus* spp. / **Yew**
Evergreen
Zones vary
Sun and part or full shade
Red autumn berries.

CHAPTER 2:
MADE FOR THE SHADE

It came as a rude surprise when I was forced to confront the dark side of the plant world. I'd moved to a shady backyard from a sunny penthouse and found that plants I'd grown easily before now only faded and died. But a serendipitous introduction to Harriet Morse (author of the 1937 classic *Gardening in the Shade*) changed the way I viewed my plot. "There *are* plants that grow in shade," this optimistic octogenarian assured me. "But it's up to you to match them with the conditions you have."

It would be nice if shade were cut and dried and labeled in a definite sort of way. But from dappled to dense, a definition can be elusive, and explanation rarely precise. Simply put, if any object comes between your plants and the sun for any significant time, the shadow it casts — however briefly — means shade. That intruding "object" may be a high wall or fence, a thick canopy of trees, a corner of a neighboring house, or even a chunk of yours.

So how to determine your conditions? Get outside and look — not once but several times. And unless your memory is better than mine, take a pencil and something sturdy on which to note the spots where the varied shadows fall, their approximate length of stay, the time of day, and the season of the year.

If, for example, you find gentle morning sun, you can grow plants that are

The cup-shaped blooms of hellebore linger in the shade from late winter through spring and sometimes into early summer.

satisfied with what I call "light" shade (for example, basil and black-eyed Susans will be fine). If you find bright, dappled sun, you can grow plants satisfied with "part" shade (like lilyturf and Japanese anemone). Throughout this book you will find plants marked for both these conditions. But the focus of this chapter is plants that manage with less. Only mushrooms grow in the *dark*. But here are the plants made for the *shade*.

PERENNIALS FOR SHADE

■ *Asarum* spp. / Wild Ginger
Hardy perennial
Zone 5
The hardy wild gingers do have spicy, fragrant stems, but don't confuse them with the tropical spice *Zingiber* used in the kitchen. But even if you can't use them for cookies, you'll love the wild gingers for their shade tolerance. My favorite is the evergreen European wild ginger *(E. europaeum)*, whose brightly polished evergreen leaves shaped like fat little hearts sit atop 4-inch stems. It was years before I noticed their tiny bell-shaped maroon flowers in spring. The deciduous native Canadian ginger *(A. canadense)* has matte, light green leaves.

■ *Convallaria majalis* / Lily-of-the-valley
Hardy perennial
Zone 4
Beloved for its white bell-shaped spring blooms, this tough plant survives remarkable levels of neglect. A steady-spreading ground cover, its tongue-shaped leaves are about a foot high. For a change of pace try 'Rosea', which has pink flowers, and 'Aureo-variegata', which has yellow-striped leaves.

■ *Epimedium* spp. / Epimedium
Hardy perennial
Zones vary
The epimediums have heart-shaped leaves that dance above 6- to 12-inch wiry stems. With rich organic soil and good moisture they'll expand their space

Clumps of Christmas fern (Polystichum acrostichoides) *add year-round texture to a mossy green scene.*

steadily. New spring leaves of most species are edged in red and in autumn turn a purple-bronze. If the nearly evergreen foliage looks ratty by winter's end, just give the plants a haircut. Flowers appear in spring, and colors include crimson *(E. rubrum),* white *(E. grandiflorum* 'White Queen'), and yellow *(E. versicolor* 'Sulphureum').

- **Ferns (Many genera and species)**

Zones vary

Too few gardeners fully appreciate the enormous variety and subtle beauty of these prehistoric plants. Their leaves — properly called fronds — come in an endless assortment of shapes, textures, and tones. Most species prefer rich soil and generous moisture. The cinnamon fern *(Osmunda cinnamomea)* gets its name

from the 2-foot-tall chocolate brown fronds that resemble cinnamon sticks. The Japanese painted fern *(Athyrium niponicum pictum)* has exquisite, silvery, serrated fronds and wine red stems. And the Christmas fern *(Polystichum acrostichoides)* is a leathery-looking evergreen.

■ *Fuchsia hybrida* / Fuchsia

Tender perennial

The many varieties of fuchsia offer gardeners a delicious assortment of mostly two-toned pink, red, white, or purple flowers that look like pendent earrings. They're spectacular in hanging baskets, but I also use them as a summer ground cover and edging for containers. Good drainage and moisture is a must. The innumerable named varieties include the double-flowered white 'Carmelita' and the lavender, blue, and pink 'Little Beauty'. My favorite is the distinctly upright, bronze-leaved 'Gartenmeister Bonstedt', whose dark orange flowers prevail in even the shadiest site.

■ *Galium odoratum* also sometimes *Asperula odorata* / Sweet Woodruff

Hardy perennial

Zone 5

Long used to flavor bowls of May wine, this neat plant has tiny oval leaves arranged like the spokes of a wheel. Most comfortable in rich, damp, slightly acid soil, these 6-inch-high plants spread slowly but steadily by runners that are easily removed if not wanted. Dainty white flowers appear in spring.

■ *Hosta* spp. / Hosta

Hardy perennial

Zones vary

It's hard to imagine a shady garden without at least one of the many hosta species or hybrids that serve so admirably for edging, accents, or just filling in. Leaves vary from broadly tall to narrow and small, with textures puckered and smooth. Leaf tones range from rich blue-grays to gold, both variegated and solid. There's likely a hosta for every taste. Long-stemmed flowers, held high above the leaves, are found on 'Elegans', 'Royal Standard', and 'Frances Williams'.

Nicely combined here with astilbe, white-edged hostas add sparkle to the shade.

■ *Impatiens wallerana* / Impatiens   *(See photo on page 85.)*

Tender perennial

A few of my snobbier garden friends (and even my own daughter) will no doubt grumble when they see I've included this plant. But for nonstop, carefree flower color in shade, these North African natives can't be beat. Breeders have given us single and double flowers in colors from white and palest pink to hot orange and purple, not to mention stripes, variegated foliage, and miniatures. Heights range to about 2 feet. Just beware the showy-leaved 'New Guinea' impatiens; this one must have sun.

The spotted leaves of lungwort (Pulmonaria saccharata), *once believed useful for curing lung diseases, combine well with woodland bloomers like fairy bells* (Disporum sessile *'Variegatum').*

■ *Lamium maculatum* and *Lamiastrum galeobdolon* / Dead Nettle

Hardy perennial

Zone 3

Not long ago, botanists listed these two plants as one, but as their differences are minimal, I'm pairing them together again. Both are superb for covering large areas of deep shade, and their rampant tendencies are useful where nothing else grows. While both reach about a foot in height, *Lamiastrum* has bright yellow spring flowers, and *Lamium*'s are pink or white. Both also include cultivars with variegated leaves. Slugs seem to adore *Lamium,* but in my garden they totally ignore the variegated *Lamiastrum* 'Herman's Pride'.

■ *Polygonatum* spp. / Solomon's-seal

Hardy perennial

Zones vary

The assorted species of Solomon's-seals have graceful arching stems, from 1 to 6 feet, which in spring are lined with small chartreuse bell-shaped flowers. In rich soil they're steady spreaders, especially if kept well watered. The variegated forms are slower to expand, but their creamy white-striped leaves add sparkle to the most forbidding corner.

■ *Pulmonaria saccharata* and *officinalis* / Lungwort

Hardy perennial

Zone 3

This is an extremely useful, slowly spreading plant whose broad, silver spotted leaves remain perky all summer. (Never mind that the 19th-century British plant explorer Reginald Farrer called them "morbid looking heaps of leprous leafage.")

*The shade-tolerant variegated Solomon's-seal (*Polygonatum odoratum *'Variegatum') has leaves edged in white and dangling white spring flowers.*

Flowers on 'Mrs. Moon' are pink fading to a purple-blue, and 'Sissinghurst White' is white and named for the white garden in Sissinghurst, England, of the early 20th-century English garden writer Vita Sackville-West.

- *Stylophorum diphyllum* / Celandine Poppy
Hardy perennial
Zone 4
The golden yellow flowers on this native perennial make their first appearance in spring and continue sporadically well into summer. The bright poppylike blooms are followed by nodding, somewhat hairy, spindle-shaped seedpods. The foot-long, downy-stemmed foliage, which vaguely resembles oak leaves, is among the first to appear after winter and the last to falter in autumn's frost. Give it good, well-drained soil and generous moisture and this steady spreader will self-sow, artistically, in unexpected corners.

- *Tiarella cordifolia* / **Foamflower**
Hardy perennial
Zone 5
A massing of foamflowers in bloom is a testament to a name well chosen. These 8-inch-tall, foamy-looking pink or white flower spikes appear in spring, rising neatly above the round, jagged leaves. Deciduous or semievergreen in cold climates, the foamflower is reliably evergreen in the South.

WOODY PLANTS FOR SHADE

- *Amelanchier* spp. / **Shadbush, Serviceberry, or Juneberry**
Deciduous shrub or small tree
Zones vary
The exquisite cloud of spring flowers (that appear when the shad fish are running) is always much too brief. But the autumn foliage color is a consolation. The two dozen species of this eastern American native include plants with either white or pink flowers.

■ *Aucuba japonica* / Gold-dust Plant or Aucuba

Evergreen shrub

Zone 7

I confess that this is not one of my favorite shrubs, but friends swear by its broad, tropical-looking leaves, which do so well in shade. More interesting are the variegated cultivars whose gold splotches and dots give the plant its common name. This is an extremely easy shrub to grow, although male and female plants are needed to ensure production of the brilliant scarlet autumn fruit.

■ *Cornus* spp. / Dogwood

Deciduous shrub or small tree

Zones vary

The dogwoods are woodland plants and manage in varying degrees of shade. The American dogwood *(C. florida)* does need some sun to set its lovely pink or white spring flowers. Unfortunately, this beautiful native has also begun to succumb at alarming rates to a fungal disease. More shade-tolerant is the Japanese or Kousa dogwood *(C. kousa)*, which also appears free of this health problem. Its white flat-topped flowers appear in early summer and by late summer become the strawberry-like fruit that birds adore. Even more shade is acceptable to the gray dogwood *(C. racemosa)*, which has white flowers too.

The pH Mystery

Understanding soil pH is not the mystery it seems. It's simply a scale, like a thermometer, with numbers from 1 to 14. The higher the number, the more alkaline the soil. The lower, the more acid. Smack in the middle, at 7, is neutral. Many popular garden plants are happiest in a slightly acid pH range, around 6. Woodland plants often do best in a more acid soil, or around 5. Herbs and veggies mostly like neutral soil, or around 7. And desert plants frequently need a more alkaline soil, or over 7.

- *Hamamelis* spp. / Witch Hazel

Deciduous shrub or small tree

Zones vary

No autumn walk is complete without a sniff of the native witch hazel *(H. virginiana)*. Yellow autumn blooms and yellow autumn foliage add to the pleasure. Hybrids from two Asian species *(H. mollis* and *H. japonica)* have expanded our witch hazel fare to include some stunning winter bloomers. Favorites include 'Arnold Promise', which greets February with a haze of aromatic yellow flowers — even with a mantle of snow — and the golden-red-blooming 'Jelana' and 'Ruby Glow'.

- *Leucothoe fontanesiana* / Leucothoe

Broad-leaved evergreen shrub

Zone 5

Graceful clusters of white flowers that strongly resemble lily-of-the-valley drape the smooth leaves of this native American through spring. Like its cousins the rhododendrons, it prefers a rich, moist, somewhat acid soil. Cultivars sporting especially colorful growth in spring include 'Rainbow', which is a coppery pink, and 'Scarletta', which is reddish purple.

- *Pieris japonica* / Andromeda or Japanese Andromeda

Broad-leaved evergreen shrub or small tree

Zone 5

Spirits are sure to be raised in even the moodiest garden by this relatively slow grower with its glossy dark green leaves. Spring brings drooping clusters of graceful, bell-shaped white flowers followed by prominent seedpods. Cultivars with pink flowers include 'Dorothy Wycoff' and 'Valley Rose'. In spring the new growth of all andromedas typically has a reddish tone but is especially eye-catching on 'Forest Flame.'

- *Rhododendron* spp. / Rhododendron and Azaleas

Hardy evergreen shrubs

Zones vary

It's impossible not to find an appealing plant among the many in the rhodo-

Spring means flowers of azalea, rhododendron, and crab apple with dots of colored tulips.
A yellow-flowered Warminster broom (Cytisus × praecox 'Warminster') grows where some
sun rays touch.

dendron genus — a group that technically includes the azaleas. With so many sizes, leaf forms, and flower colors to choose from, decision-making can be a headache, and unreliable nursery labels add confusion. To be sure of getting the flower color you want, buy plants only when they're in bloom. Moist, rich, somewhat acid soil is essential. For serious shade, stick to the evergreen rhododendron. The many beautiful deciduous species need more sun.

■ *Taxus* spp. / Yew
Needle evergreen shrub
Zones vary
Seemingly never changing, the many species and cultivars of these brooding evergreens are remarkably tolerant of neglect and creative (or clumsy) pruning. In autumn, the soft needles of female plants are dotted by bright red pea-sized berries (whose seed is poisonous). The English yews *(T. baccada)* include 'Rependens', a low, flat-topped shrub. The Japanese yews *(T. cuspidata)* include 'Jeffrey's Pyramidal', shaped as its name implies. And the Intermediate yews *(T. media)* include the popular, stiffly upright 'Hicksii'.

ADDITIONAL PLANTS FOR SHADE

■ *Astilbe* spp. / Astilbe
Hardy perennial
Zones vary
In summer, 1- to 3-foot-tall spiky-looking flowers in pink, lavender, red, or white gracefully rise above ferny foliage.

■ *Caladium bicolor* / Caladium *(See photo on page 10.)*
Tender bulb
See page 83.

Pale peach plumes of astilbe brighten the shade near a cluster of stately purple alliums.

Beebalm (Monarda), *Ligularia, Thalictrum, and bugbane* (Cimicifuga) *are happiest when their shady home also has moist soil.*

■ *Cimicifuga racemosa* / **Snakeroot**

Hardy perennial

Zone 4

The white fuzzy-looking flower spikes that rise above the foliage in summer grow between 4 and 6 feet tall. They remain through winter as dark pearls along the stately stems.

■ *Coleus blumei* / **Coleus** *(See photo on page 105.)*

Tender perennial

The many foliage shapes of coleus are splashed in hues of red, purple, white, yellow, or green. Purple flower spikes appear in summer.

- *Helleborus niger* and *H. orientalis* / **Christmas Rose and Lenten Rose**

Hardy evergreen perennial

Zones vary

Although extremely poisonous if ingested, these handsome plants produce long-lasting cup-shaped flowers more or less in time for the season of their name.

- *Hypoestes phyllostachya* / **Polka-dot Plant**

Tender perennial

Small, oval-shaped leaves, spotted rose pink, lavender, white, or red, densely cover the trailing stems.

- *Tricyrtis hirta* / **Toad Lily**

Hardy perennial

Zone 6

In late summer, tiny orchidlike flowers in white, yellow, or mauve snuggle atop arching 2-foot-high stems.

- *Tsuga canadensis* / **Canadian Hemlock**

Hardy evergreen tree

Zone 4

Small shiny needles that are green above and striped a silver-blue beneath line the hemlock's gracefully drooping limbs.

- *Vinca minor* / **Myrtle, Common Periwinkle**

Hardy evergreen perennial

Zone 4

These trailing stems make a thick carpet that's useful for covering walls, rocks, and bare soil. Light blue or white flowers appear in spring and sometimes sporadically through summer.

- *Viola* spp. / **Violets**

Hardy perennials and annuals

Zones vary

This old-fashioned flowering group has charming white, purple, yellow, or pink blooms that appear in spring. Sweet violet *(V. odorata)* is the aromatic bloomer favored by florists.

Chapter 3:
Some Like It Wet

If you want to put your nongardening friends to sleep, just discuss your problems with soil, that stuff your plants must sink their roots in. The "ideal" is a fluffy, crumblike loam that water drains through with sensible efficiency. But because of their composition or location, some soils never seem to dry out at all.

With time and hard work (not to mention lots of money for subsurface changes) you may succeed in alleviating your soggy condition, at least in a limited area. But rather than curse your waterlogged site, give it a romantic name and find the plants whose nature enables them to live there happily.

Creative choices for name changes include bog, swamp, marsh, and wet meadow. Labels like these will not only make you feel better, but are in fact legitimate — even desirable — garden terms. (Politicians aren't the only folks who can put a good spin on a bad situation and come out ahead.) A bog is a wetland whose water level rarely changes, and where a generous amount of peat encourages the growth of certain acid-loving plants. A swamp is a low-lying area that is home to water-tolerant trees and shrubs. Marshes are distinguished by their many herbaceous species, while a wet meadow is a kind of grassland with intermittent waterlogged soil. It makes little difference if you're not sure which category your damp landscape fits into; here are some plants that, to varying degrees, do like it wet.

The cardinal flower (Lobelia cardinalis) *needs moist soil for a good crop of its late-summer red flowers.*

Marsh marigold (Caltha palustris) *bears its luminous blooms in spring and disappears underground in summer's heat.*

PERENNIALS FOR MOIST SOIL

■ *Adiantum pedatum* / Maidenhair Fern
Hardy perennial
Zone 4
Part or full shade
Dainty, light green leaflets arranged in a fan-shaped pattern top the brittle purple-black stems of this winsome American native. Typically found in moist woodlands, it spreads slowly by underground stems that creep horizontally just beneath the soil. Height varies between 1 and 2 feet.

■ *Caltha palustris* / Marsh Marigold
Hardy perennial
Zone 4
Sun or part shade
It's easy to mistake the bright yellow spring flowers of marsh marigold for its cousin, the buttercup. Since this plant disappears during its resting period in

summer, it's ideal for a swampy area that dries in late summer, when it's at rest. A less-hardy white form *C. p.* 'Alba', a native of North India, flowers earlier and is more compact.

■ *Carex* spp. / Sedge
Hardy perennial
Zones vary
Sun and part or full shade

This large genus of grasslike plants includes many with handsome foliage. Some are well behaved and remain in neat clumps. Others quickly ramble across the landscape. In my garden, *Carex ornithopoda* 'Variegata' is a restrained grower with exquisite narrow leaves striped pale yellow and green that are maybe 5 inches tall. The variegated form, Morrow's sedge *(C. morrowii),* grows to about a foot, and its $1/4$-inch leaves are striped with white. If rapid growth is needed, look for the variegated river sedge (*C. riparia* 'Variegata'), and site it where its roots will always be moist.

■ *Chelone glabra* / Turtlehead
Hardy perennial
Zone 3
Sun or part shade

Crowded clusters of peculiar white or greenish yellow flowers — which do indeed look like tiny turtle heads — top the stiff 3-foot stems. This plant's late-summer blooms last through early fall. A pink species *(C. lyonii)* blooms even later and tolerates more shade. In my garden, turtlehead tolerates soil that is intermittently dry, but I suspect it doesn't like it much.

The curious blooms of pink turtlehead (Chelone lyonii) *line stiffly upright stems, which are at their best in moist soil.*

The bright flowers of yellow flag (Iris pseudocorus), *also known as water iris, color a pond.*

■ *Equisetum hymenale* / Horsetail
Hardy evergreen perennial
Zone 5
Sun or part shade
Like those of ferns and ginkgos, the ancestors of these elegant grassy-looking plants date from the time of the dinosaurs. The hollow-jointed, segmented stems have no leaves or obvious flowers, but the strongly vertical silhouette contrasts well with other species. Give them the marshy conditions they love and they will romp rapidly (very!) across the landscape. In my garden they remain neatly in place, but only because the surrounding soil is too dry for their taste.

■ *Iris pseudocorus* / Yellow Flag
Hardy perennial
Zone 5
Sun or light shade
Bright yellow early-summer flowers distinguish this adaptable member of the beardless iris group whose rich green, swordlike leaves quickly form large clumps. It is remarkable in its acceptance of soils that range from seriously soggy (mine

is in a pot in a pond) to nearly dry (the pot comes out at the season's end). 'Variegata' has leaves striped pale yellow and green.

■ *Ligularia dentata* / **Ligularia**

Hardy perennial

Zone 5

Part shade

In constantly moist soil, the handsome umbrella-like leaves of ligularia will flourish and not droop depressingly as they invariably do in "normal" garden soil. Do go classic and pair 'Desdemona' (whose young leaves are wine red or purple) with the larger 'Othello'. The narrow-spiked ligularia *(L. stenocephala)* has jagged-edged leaves and graceful, tall, bright gold flowers. The blooms of 'The Rocket' are a paler yellow.

■ *Lobelia cardinalis* / **Cardinal Flower** *(See photo on page 32.)*

Hardy perennial

Zone 2

Sun or part shade

Maybe it's because I'm a city kid, but I've never forgotten those red wands waving at me — or so it seemed — from the edge of the pond at the New England Wildflower Society's Garden in the Woods, in Framingham, Massachusetts. They were cardinal flowers swaying gently in the breeze. The 2- to 3-foot-tall flower spikes color summer's end and last into early autumn. A cousin, the great blue lobelia *(L. siphilitica),* has purple flowers with a blue lip with white stripes and blooms for a somewhat shorter time.

■ *Primula sieboldii* / **Primrose** *(See photo on page 38.)*

Hardy perennial

Zone 5

Part shade

Flat-topped, funnel-shaped flowers in shades of red, pink, magenta, and white

---

TIPS FOR SUCCESS

SLUG THOSE SLUGS

It is possible to control the slimy creatures called slugs without poisons. I cover them with a spoonful of undiluted water-soluble fertilizer (like Miracle-Gro), or I simply jump on them. Those who are squeamish (or those not yet sufficiently angry) can also keep slugs at bay by covering the soil around afflicted plants with a rough material they won't cross, such as wood ashes, finely ground eggshells, or diatomaceous earth (a commercial product derived from the sharp fossil remains of prehistoric algae).

A marshy spring woodland becomes a golden pond with primrose, yellow flag, and marsh marigold.

cover these charming Japanese natives from spring through early summer. Their resting period begins in late summer when the crinkly gray-green leaves disappear underground and drier soil is tolerated.

- *Rodgersia* spp. / Rodgersia
Hardy perennial
Zones vary
Part shade
This large foliage plant — somewhat tropical in appearance — definitely is not for everyone. But if you have space, do give it a try. The variously shaped leaves are an especially handsome edging for a stream, wet meadow, or pond. The stems of *R. podophylla* grow to about 5 feet, and its 10-inch leaves are colored a metallic bronze. *R. tabularis* is shorter with scalloped foliage.

WOODY PLANTS FOR MOIST SOILS

■ *Acer rubrum* / **Swamp Maple**

Tree

Zone 1

Sun or light shade

Blood-red early spring flowers and scarlet autumn color give this native American part of its common name, while the other describes its favorite site. A rapid grower, it quickly achieves its mature height of 60 feet. As such, the swamp maple is a useful shade tree, willingly tolerant of alternate wet and dry soils. The ridged bark and silvery gray limbs add a handsome touch in winter.

■ *Amelanchier laevis* / **Shadbush**

Shrub or small tree

Zone 4

Sun and part or full shade

The sublime cloud of white spring flowers that appear on this plant (when the shad fish swim upstream) is always too brief. The birds adore the tasty blue berries, but even when they disappear, you will still enjoy the orange-gold autumn leaves and multistemmed vaselike winter outline. *A. grandiflora* 'Autumn Brilliance' is more treelike in shape and has orange-red fall leaves.

■ *Andromeda glaucophylla* / **Bog Rosemary**

Evergreen shrub

Zone 2

Sun

Years ago I tried this absolutely enchanting plant only to watch it die in a painfully short time. My mistake was too much shade and too little moisture for a plant that grows wild in the wet, acid soils from Virginia to Manitoba. Its tiny narrow leaves and petite dimensions — rarely more than a foot high — make it a favorite of rock gardeners. Clusters of pink or white bell-shaped flowers appear in early summer. A somewhat larger version is *A. polifolia,* a cousin that will tolerate a bit more shade, but not less moisture.

TIPS FOR SUCCESS

LOVE THAT MANURE

Don't be fooled by the relatively low fertilizer percentages of NPK listed on packages of natural manures (cow, horse, chicken, and so on). Unlike chemical fertilizers, the value of manure lies in its ability to enrich the soil with organic matter that is the basis for truly good growing. Manures improve the soil structure, increase its oxygen content and ability to hold moisture, and, most important, create an environment conducive to the growth of beneficial microorganisms.

■ *Betula nigra* / River Birch
Tree
Zone 3
Sun

As its name implies, this native American is most at home at the edge of streams or other low areas where its roots can easily reach water. The silvery gold or red-brown bark peels and curls in narrow strips, adding handsome two-toned winter texture. A quick grower — maybe 40 feet in 20 years — this tree appears to be immune to the bronze birch borer, a serious pest for its more sensitive relatives.

■ *Cornus sericea* or *stolonifera* / Red-osier Dogwood
Shrub
Zone 2
Sun or light shade

Travel the Massachusetts Turnpike and you'll see a roadside medley of varieties of this native shrub. Typically found in eastern American swamps, its bright red- or yellow-hued stems are most vivid in winter when seen against snow. Color is brightest on the newest twigs. 'Isanti' has vivid red stems and grows to about 5 feet in height. 'Silver & Gold' has yellow twigs and variegated leaves, topping out between 8 and 10 feet. The dwarf 'Kelseyi' has red stems that grow only about 2 feet high.

■ *Rhododendron viscosum* / Swamp Azalea
Shrub or small tree
Zone 4
Part shade

The intensely fragrant white flowers of this deciduous azalea are a welcome mid-summer sight. An American native found in swamps from the Carolinas to Maine, its small leaves glow orange-bronze in autumn. Height varies from 9 to about 15 feet.

ADDITIONAL PLANTS FOR MOIST SOILS

■ *Clethra alnifolia* / Summersweet
See page 97.

- *Dryopteris goldiana* / Goldie's Fern or Giant Wood Fern

Hardy perennial

Zone 3

Part or full shade

Under its preferred conditions — a cool, humusy, swamp — the stately dark green fronds of this native fern may stretch to 5 feet in height.

- *Eupatorium maculatum* / Joe-Pye Weed

Hardy perennial

Zone 3

Sun or light shade

In late summer these 6- to 10-foot-high marsh-loving plants are topped with fluffy purple-pink flowers. These blooms are also sumptuous in fresh arrangements or dried.

In moist soil, the fluffy flowers of Joe-Pye weed are late-summer showstoppers.

- *Salix matsudana* 'Tortuosa' / Corkscrew Willow

Shrub or small tree

Zone 4

Sun or part shade

Unusual twisted or contorted branches make this rapid grower an outstanding specimen both in the winter landscape and in fresh flower arrangements.

- *Symplocarpus foetidus* / Skunk Cabbage

Hardy perennial

Zone 4

Part or full shade

If bruised, this swamp plant emits an unfortunate pungent scent. The curious Jack-in-the-pulpit flowers precede the huge oval leaves, signaling winter's end.

- *Viola lanceolata* / Lance-leaved Violet

Hardy perennial

Zone 3

Sun or part shade

Its common name aptly describes the spear-shaped leaves of this bog or wet-meadow plant whose white spring or early-summer flowers have hints of blue.

Chapter 4:

And Some Like It Hot and Dry

At first blush, it seems inconceivable that any gardener would complain about luxuriant sun and warmth. But when the result is a garden that's ever hot and dry, watering becomes a full-time chore and the fun begins to fade. Such a challenge confronts those who plant in an arid climate or in any exposed site, and this includes containers on a sun-drenched rooftop, terrace, balcony, patio, or deck.

Since the only plants that need *no* water are plastic, live plants with minimum water needs have gained in popularity. Many of these species can be detected by their thick or fleshy stems and leaves, light or silvery foliage, glossy or leathery leaves, or nap of fine hairs. Such plants not only save gardeners work and time, but help them realize their civic responsibility as water consumption rises and reservoirs fall.

Planting species amenable to water rationing even has an official name — xeriscaping — from the Greek word *xeros,* which means dry. (Actually, the xeriscaping movement first gained momentum some years ago in Denver, Col-

The Vitex agnus-castus, *a deciduous shrub or small tree, has deliciously fragrant foliage and flowers.*

orado, when landscapers worked with the water department to develop more conservation-oriented plantings.)

Along with choosing appropriate species, serious xeriscapers also discovered anew the importance of a protective mulch (that is, covering the soil with an organic shield such as shredded bark, buckwheat hulls, hay, or leaves) and the importance of the most efficient irrigation system (such as the soaker hose or low-volume dripper).

Here are some plants to grow in areas that are mostly hot and dry, or where conserving liquid assets is essential.

Perennials for Where It's Hot and Dry

■ *Achillea millefolium* / **Yarrow**
Hardy perennial
Zone 4
Sun
Named for the Greek god Achilles, whose wounds it puportedly healed, this genus includes many easily grown species. Most have aromatic gray-green leaves and reach a height of around 3 feet. Flower colors vary from crimson to cream. 'Lavender Deb' has finely cut foliage and pale lavender summer flowers. 'Paprika' has flat, ruby red flowers that remain into early fall. 'Moonshine' has canary yellow blooms.

■ *Echinops ritro* / **Globe Thistle**
Hardy perennial
Zone 3
Sun or light shade
The foliage has unpleasant prickles, but I can never resist gathering long-stemmed bunches of these metallic purple-blue flowers for late-summer arrangements. The globe-shaped blooms, borne on tough, 2- to 4-foot-tall plants with gray-green leaves, are also good for drying. 'Taplow Blue' is a steel blue with 2-inch balls; the flowers of 'Veitch's Blue' are darker and smaller.

Golden yarrow, pale lavender scabiosa, and maroon Mexican hat (Ratibida columnifera) *are a natural bouquet in a hot, dry garden.*

■ *Euphorbia* spp. / Spurge

Tender and hardy perennials

Sun

The members of this group emit a milky sap that can irritate skin, so some gardeners shy away from planting them. But that's a shame, since the spurges offer a handsome assortment, typically with sulfur yellow flowers and gray-green foliage. I'm especially fond of *E. polychroma*, an upright plant that is hardy to Zone 4. *E. myrsinites* has more trailing stems and is hardy to Zone 5.

Baby's-breath (Gypsophila paniculata) *is a dainty foil for* Coreopsis verticillata.

■ *Gypsophila paniculata* / Baby's-breath

Hardy perennial

Zone 4

Sun

A fluffy mass of baby's-breath flowers always reminds me of a bridal bouquet. The plant's numerous slender stems are dotted with gray-green narrow leaves and grow to about 3 feet high and wide. In summer they're covered with the tiny white or pink blooms. 'Compacta Plena' has white double flowers, 'Pink Star' is pale pink, and *G. repens* is a mat-forming creeping species.

■ *Helichrysum* spp. / Everlastings

Tender perennials and shrubs

Sun or light shade

The many species and hybrids of everlastings are sun-loving, drought-tolerant plants that vary in size and shape. Most of these daisy family members bear summer flowers in a range that spans from white, yellow, and orange, to red, violet, and brown. The curry plant *(H. angustifolium)* has tiny silvery gray leaves and a distinct curry aroma that I find overwhelming. The blooms of strawflower *(H. bracteatum)* are excellent for dried bouquets, and *H. splendidum* is a striking 3-foot-high shrub with white woolly leaves.

■ *Nipponanthemum nipponicum* or *Chrysanthemum nipponicum* / **Nippon or Montauk Daisy**

Hardy perennial
Zone 5
Sun
Clean white flowers in late summer and glossy dark green leaves make this plant a favorite near the shore. So popular is it on the eastern end of Long Island that most gardeners there know it only as Montauk daisy, named after the popular fishing town. In mild climates, this plant acts more like a shrub than a perennial. To ensure good blooms, cut the woody stems to the ground in early spring.

■ *Senecio cineraria* / **Dusty Miller**

Tender perennial
Sun or light shade
Many plants are sold under the "Dusty Miller" moniker, and all have silvery leaves, with either finely cut or lacy-looking foliage. Usually treated as an annual, this is actually a tender shrubby perennial that can reach about 2 feet tall in mild climates. I use the gray textured foliage in flower arrangements.

■ *Yucca filamentosa* / **Adam's Needle**

Hardy evergreen perennial
Zone 5
Sun
This native of Central America resembles a giant porcupine and adds an elegant architectural silhouette that contrasts well with other garden shapes. Its 2- to 3-

'Blue Rug' junipers, Cotoneaster horizontalis, *and low-growing sedums enjoy a hot and dry rocky terrain.*

foot-long sword-shaped blue-green leaves have sharp tips and loose, hairlike fibers along the edge. In midsummer, the stiffly upright "needle" of large white flowers makes its appearance and lingers through winter. 'Bright Edge' and 'Variegata' have variegated leaves but are somewhat less hardy.

WOODY PLANTS FOR WHERE IT'S HOT AND DRY

■ *Caryopteris clandonensis* / **Blue Spirea or Bluebeard**
Deciduous shrub
Zone 5
Sun
I remember first seeing this plant in a nursery and wondering if the price included the butterflies that seemed glued to its fluffy lavender-blue blooms. Its

downy gray-green leaves contrast well with the late-summer flower clusters. Rarely topping 2 to 3 feet, this plant should be cut to the ground in early spring to encourage vigorous blooming stems. Cultivars include 'Blue Mist', a delicate powder blue, and 'Dark Knight', which is more compact and more purple.

■ *Gleditsia triacanthos* / **Honey Locust**

Tree

Zone 4

Sun or part shade

The honey locust's delicate, ferny-looking foliage and graceful open silhouette makes for the barest of shade. I especially like the curly seedpods that dangle until they darken and drop in autumn when the neighborhood children greedily scoop them up. The tiny autumn leaves — a bright yellow — remain only briefly on the tree and melt away just as quickly on the ground. Cultivars include 'Sunburst', whose young leaves are golden yellow, and 'Skyline', which is more pyramidal in outline.

■ *Lantana camara* / **Lantana**

Tender shrub

Sun or light shade

The multicolored flowers in red, pink, yellow, or white are followed by black berries (which are poisonous). Although it's never happened to me, an allergic reaction may be experienced by those who are sensitive to its rough, pungent foliage. In my New York City window box, lantana continues its flowering until the first serious frost.

■ *Lavandula* spp. / **Lavender** *(See photo on page 50.)*

Hardy and tender shrubs

Zones vary

Sun

I'm one of those who is absolutely intoxicated by the heady scent of lavender. The many species and varieties typically have aromatic gray-green fuzzy foliage on bushy plants that grow between 1 and 3 feet high. Fragrant pale purple flower

---

TIPS FOR SUCCESS

GRAY WATER

Do your share for water conservation by using kitchen "gray water" for your plants. This is waste water that's not contaminated by cleansers or grease. Keep a pail near your sink to collect the water used to rinse fruit or veggies, boil eggs, or thaw frozen food packets. Also, catch and use what runs from the hot-water tap before the heated water appears.

A gravel and wood path is lined with yellow-flowering santolina, thyme, and lavender.

spikes appear in summer. *L. angustifolia* 'Munstead' is an early bloomer. *L. a.* 'Hidcote' is a dark purple. And the French lavender *L. dentata candicans* has exquisite, finely cut, ferny-looking foliage. These are all hardy to Zone 5.

■ *Vitex agnus-castus* / **Chaste Tree** *(See photo on page 42.)*
Deciduous shrub or small tree
Zone 6
Sun
The foliage of this rapid grower is dark green above and a silvery green below. If crushed, the leaves emit a spicy fragrance. The long narrow clusters of fragrant purple flowers flourish in summer heat. Usually multistemmed, in milder climates these plants may grow as large as 10 to 20 feet high and wide.

ADDITIONAL PLANTS THAT LIKE IT HOT AND DRY

(Also see plants in chapter 5, "Gusts, Blasts, Breezes, and Big Winds," page 55.)

■ *Asclepias tuberosa* / Butterfly Weed
Hardy perennial
Zone 3
Sun

The bright orange summer blooms of this native plant do indeed attract butter-flies. They are also good cut flowers, and trimming inspires repeat blooms.

The sun-loving butterfly weed (Asclepias tuberosa) *has waxy, upward-facing flowers.*

■ *Berberis* spp. / Barberry
Evergreen and deciduous shrubs
Zones vary
Sun

The many barberry species vary in shape from upright to spreading and are mostly spiny. The yellow flowers are followed by red, yellow, or black fruit.

African daisies (Gazania hybrids), geranium, and prostrate junipers revel in the heat of this large terrace. Their containers are 18 inches wide but only 4 inches high.

- *Festuca ovina* var. *glauca* / Blue Fescue

Hardy grass

Zone 4

Sun

This ornamental grass grows about 10 inches high and remains a dense mound. Summer brings wheat-colored flower plumes to contrast with its slender blue-green leaves.

- *Gazania* hybrids / Gazania or African Daisy

Annual

These spectacular natives of South Africa, members of the daisy family, only open in full sun. Colors vary from yellow and orange to pink and red.

- *Gomphrena globosa* / Globe Amaranth

Tender perennial

Sun or light shade

The tiny globe-shaped flowers in white, purple, pink, or orange top bushy 1- to 2-foot-tall plants. Dry them for use later as Christmas trimming.

- *Sedum* 'Autumn Joy' / Sedum 'Autumn Joy'

Hardy perennial

Zone 3

Sun

The aptly named sedum 'Autumn Joy' has succulent stems that are topped in late summer with fuzzy flowers. As autumn progresses, the blooms change from glowing pink to rusty red.

Sedum 'Autumn Joy' bears its heat-resistant flowers in late summer.

- *Verbascum* spp. / Mullein

Hardy biennial and perennial

Zones vary

Sun

The stately spikes of tiny pale yellow or white flowers may rise as much as 6 feet tall. Foliage typically is a woolly gray-green.

CHAPTER 5:

GUSTS, BLASTS, BREEZES, AND BIG WINDS

Some landscapes are so windswept that few plants can manage and people would rather not. Wind can reduce flourishing plants to naked stems and bend or break limbs. Wind means rapid desiccation or the continual loss of moisture from leaves. Wilting and eventually death occurs when the roots are unable to absorb and replace the lost moisture quickly enough to satisfy the plant's system.

From mountain to prairie, fierce winds may be part of any open landscape and may change at whim from a soft breeze to a vicious gale. Certainly this is true for the shore garden, where wind resistance — and salt resistance — is essential. It is also true for the rooftop garden. Rooftop gardeners should give their plants the largest containers they have room for, thereby providing maximum space in which to store moisture and to firmly anchor roots.

You can't stop the wind, but you can choose plants whose nature allows them to survive. Here are some plants with a known ability to shrug off gusts, blasts, breezes, and other big winds.

A symphony of coreopsis, Russian sage (Perovskia atriplicifolia), *lamb's-ears* (Stachys byzantina), *and blue fescue* (Festuca cinera) *flourishes in a sunny site.*

Daylilies, like the long-blooming 'Stella de Oro', welcome each day with a new spray of flowers.

PERENNIALS FOR WINDSWEPT AREAS

■ *Coreopsis verticillata* / **Coreopsis** *(See photo on page 54.)*
Hardy perennial
Zone 3
Sun or light shade
The airy-looking coreopsis has loose clusters of small daisylike flowers. Although sometimes slow to reappear in spring, it's well worth the wait. 'Golden Showers' has rich yellow flowers, while those of 'Moonbeam' are pale yellow. Shear the spent flowers to encourage new blooms. Late-season flowers left to set seed become dark brown pods that linger through winter.

■ *Hemerocallis* **hybrids / Daylily**
Hardy perennial
Zones vary
Sun or part shade
Each summer's day a new crop of spectacular flowers covers these grassy-leaved clumps. Daylilies are delightfully free of insects and diseases and come in an assortment of colors that range from deep red to salmon pink, orange, rose, and lavender, with bicolors too. The golden 'Stella de Oro' is a long-flowering favorite, but with hundreds of hybrids to choose from, decision-making can be a challenge.

A graceful clump of maiden grass Miscanthus sinensis *'Morning Light' is a smooth backdrop for black-eyed Susan* (Rudbeckia nitida).

■ *Miscanthus sinensis* / Maiden Grass

Hardy perennial

Zone 5

Sun or light shade

With time, this beautiful ornamental grass expands to resemble a grand and graceful fountain. The narrow, arching leaves grow from 5 to 8 feet tall and add a musical note as they move in the wind. The feathery silver-pink plumes appear in late summer and remain through winter. 'Gracillimus' is one of several favorite cultivars. 'Yakushima' is a dwarf with dark green leaves. 'Variegatus' has cream and white stripes.

■ *Portulaca grandiflora* / Portulaca or Moss Rose

Annual

Sun

Its common name notwithstanding, this nearly nonstop summer bloomer is neither a moss nor a rose. It is instead a succulent flower from Brazil whose fleshy stems and leaves are mostly prostrate. It is also a rainbow of flowers on sunny summer days when covered with its many pink, yellow, red, purple, or white roselike flowers. In my rooftop garden it was also a colorful cascade over the container edges. The inch-wide flowers close at night and stay closed if the day is cloudy.

Woody Plants for Windswept Areas

■ *Berberis thunbergii* / Japanese Barberry

Shrub

Zone 4

Sun or light shade

The nasty little spines on this otherwise delightful plant should keep neighbors' children (and other mischief-makers) at bay. One of the first plants to leaf out in spring, it has early yellow flowers and bright green summer foliage. Autumn brings shades of scarlet, orange, or purple-red. The bright red autumn fruit lasts well into winter. The many notable hybrids include several red-leaf forms like 'Crimson Pygmy' and 'Rose Glow'. 'Aurea' has golden leaves. Unfortunately, this adaptive Asian native is now taking over old-fields and woodlands and is best confined to town gardens where it can't escape.

■ *Caragana arborescens* / Siberian Pea Tree

Shrub or small tree

Zone 2

Sun or light shade

This exceptionally tough plant from Siberia is also exceptionally decorative with small, snapdragon-like yellow flowers in spring. A cascade of light green leaves, typical of its cousins in the pea family, lines its graceful limbs. My favorite is the weeping form, *C. a.* 'Pendula', an especially striking accent for a windy corner.

A single clump of plumed grasses whisper in the wind.

■ *Cytisus × praecox* 'Warminster' / **Broom** *(See photo on page 27.)*
Shrub
Zone 6
Sun or light shade
My first encounter with this plant was in a sheltered backyard, so it was quite a surprise to find it thriving along exposed, windy roadsides. An unusual-looking shrub, with slender, angled, light green twigs, it is a marvelous contrast with everything else in the garden. In spring, pealike flowers in yellow, cream, or purple completely cover the 3- to 5-foot-tall stems. 'Allgold' has bright yellow late-spring flowers, and 'Hollandia' has two-tone flowers in pink and white.

The wind-resistant autumn berries or "hips" of the Rugosa rose last well into winter if not harvested for jellies.

■ *Potentilla fruticosa* / Bush Cinquefoil
Shrub
Zone 4
Sun
This twiggy shrub, with leaves that resemble those of strawberries, is surprisingly resistant to wind. After a first flush, the small rose-shaped flowers continue through much of summer. Known primarily for its bright yellow or white flowers, breeding and selection have expanded the shades to include orange, red, and pink.

■ *Rosa rugosa* / Rugosa Rose
Shrub
Sun or light shade
Those not familiar with the versatility of roses may be surprised to learn that this huge genus includes many rugged species that withstand some truly impos-

sible conditions. A favorite for wind and shore areas is the Rugosa rose (sometimes called the beach rose or salt-spray rose), which stands 2 to 5 feet tall. It has upright fuzzy stems, fragrant pink or white flowers, and bright orange-red berries ("hips") in autumn.

■ *Tamarix ramosissima* / **Tamarisk**
Shrub
Zone 6
Sun
The limbs of this wispy-looking shrub are covered with scalelike blue-gray foliage that is less than an $\frac{1}{8}$ inch long. These hug the twigs so tightly the plant looks leafless. The feathery branches move gracefully in the wind, offering not a whit of resistance. Maximum height is about 10 feet, and the pink flowers appear in summer.

ADDITIONAL PLANTS FOR WINDSWEPT SPACES

(Also see plants in chapter 4, "And Some Like It Hot and Dry," page 43.)

■ *Calluna vulgaris* / **Heather**
Subshrub
Zone 4
Sun
Clouds of tiny white, pink, or purple flowers cover these 2-foot-tall evergreens from midsummer through autumn.

■ *Erigeron glaucus* / **Beach Aster**
Perennial
Zone 3
Sun or light shade
From spring through fall, pale purple daisylike flowers blanket these spreading clumps of dark green leaves.

> **TIPS FOR SUCCESS**
>
> **DON'T RUSH SPRING**
>
> Don't let those first balmy spring days fool you into too-early planting of summer seedlings. Wait until nighttime temperatures stabilize around 65°F before setting out tender types like basil and tomatoes. Only cool-weather plants, like pansies, lettuce, and peas, enjoy chilly early spring nights.

*A wind-resistant planting of striped eulalia grass (*Miscanthus sinensis *'Variegatus')* *has flower accents of yarrow (*Achillea millefolium*).*

■ *Myrica pensylvanica* / **Bayberry**
Shrub
Zone 4
Sun
This is the plant whose silvery gray berries (on female plants only) are used for aromatic candles.

■ *Perovskia atriplicifolia* / **Russian Sage** *(See photo on page 54.)*
See page 95.

■ *Phalaris arundinacea* 'Picta' / **Ribbon Grass**
Grass
Zone 4
Sun or part shade
The spreading patches of 2- to 3-foot-tall stems make good ground covers and soil stabilizers. The narrow leaves are striped white and green.

■ *Santolina chamaecyparissus* / Lavender Cotton also Gray Santolina
Hardy perennial
Zone 6
Sun
These bushy 2-foot-high mounds of fragrant, silvery gray leaves produce their small yellow flowers in summer.

■ *Solidago sempervirens* / Seaside Goldenrod
Hardy perennial
Zone 5
Sun
This coastal native wildflower has sturdy 2- to 6-foot-tall stems and bright yellow autumn flowers.

■ *Thymus* **spp.** / **Thyme** *(See photo on page 78.)*
See page 79.

HEDGING YOUR WIND

You can't stop the wind, but you can convert those tumultuous gusts to a manageable breeze with a windbreak barrier or hedge. Clipped or unclipped, a hedge tempers the wind even as it adds a polite screen for neighbors and passersby. Where possible, combine evergreen and deciduous species, planting them fairly close and in multiple rows if there's room.

Use the following plants singly, or mix and match them in a hedgerow as a windbreak barrier that is also a screen for privacy.

■ *Elaeagnus angustifolia* / **Russian Olive**
Shrub or small tree
Zone 2
Sun and light shade
Even in poor soil and violent winds, the silvery gray-green leaves of the Russian olive quickly form a thick misty cloud, which can be an advantage or disadvantage, depending on where it's used. In gardens near wildlands, it has escaped and

taken over nearby shores and meadows. I used it without guilt on my windy city terrace. In spring, small yellow flowers line the stems and form the silvery fruit by autumn. Russian olives can reach their full height of about 15 feet fairly quickly, and the young branches may have long thorns. The autumn olive *(E. umbellata)* is shorter and bushier, with the silvery tone on the leaf undersides only.

■ *Juniperus virginiana* / **Eastern Redcedar**
Needle evergreen tree or shrub
Zone 2
Sun

The aromatic source of cedar chests and closets, the eastern redcedar is also valued for its resistance to wind. The bark is a handsome red-brown that peels or exfoliates for a wonderfully rich texture. Maximum height can be about 30 feet. The many cultivars include the pyramidal 'Canaertii', which has dark bronze-green foliage, and the bushy 'Kosteri', whose gray-blue needles have a hint of purple.

■ *Ligustrum* **spp.** / **Privet**
Evergreen or semievergreen shrubs or small trees
Zones vary
Sun or part shade

The tough privets are fast-growing shrubs that quickly stretch to their limit of 18 feet. But since they're so amenable to severe trimming, they are often kept from reaching their ultimate height. As a result, few gardeners experience the intensely sweet, creamy white late-spring flowers that top uncut twigs, or get to see birds diving after the black late-summer berries. Among the several golden-leaf hybrids are *L. vulgare* 'Lodense', a tough bushy plant that grows only about 4 feet, and *L. vicaryi,* which is more than double that height.

■ *Pinus nigra* / **Austrian Pine**
Evergreen tree
Zone 4
Sun

This is a medium- to fast-growing evergreen that can reach 60 feet in height. Somewhat cylindrical when young, it looks more like an umbrella with age. Its

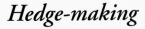

Hedge-making

It's never too late to start a hedge. Yard gardeners should prepare for planting by digging a trench or a straight line of holes using a hose as linear guide. Rooftop gardeners should partially fill several large containers with a blend of equal parts topsoil, perlite, and peat moss. For each plant to be added, stir in a heaping shovelful of cow manure and two handfuls of a granular 5-10-5 fertilizer. When the plants are in place, form a shallow depression around their bases to collect moisture.

---

long stiff needles are a shiny dark green. The many hybrids include 'Aurea', whose young shoots have gold-toned needles.

■ *Populus tremuloides* / **Quaking Aspen**
Deciduous tree
Zone 1
Sun or light shade
A stunning sight in autumn, when its yellow leaves flutter in the slightest breeze, the quaking aspen is a member of the poplar family. A fast grower that can reach 40 feet, it is a tough American native that tolerates a wide range of soils. It actually grows wild from Mexico to Alaska. Young plants are somewhat pyramidal in outline and rounder with age, and the smooth, greenish cream-colored bark grows rougher as the tree matures.

■ *Taxus cuspidata* / **Japanese Yew**
Evergreen shrub or small tree
Zone 4
Sun and part or full shade
This versatile, slow-growing evergreen, with lustrous, flat dark green needles, manages to withstand an extraordinary range of trying conditions, and wind is one of them. Choose from among the many upright or spreading forms. 'Capitata' can reach a height of about 40 feet and has a bronze hue in winter. 'Nana' tends to be mostly short and fat and eventually grows 20 feet tall.

Chapter 6:
Ground Covers for Hiding Dirt or Saving a Slope

Ground covers are not lowly plants. They're marvelous spreading species that, when grown together, gracefully decorate bare soil, blanket the feet of leggy shrubs and tall perennials, brighten the base of majestic trees, and hold eroding hillsides in place.

Ground covers eliminate the need for boring mulches and exhausting lawns. They minimize weeding and reduce the evaporation of moisture as they shade the roots of their fellow plants. They also camouflage the messy ripening leaves of spring bulbs that can hang around for weeks.

And, as "crack fillers" (as my husband calls them), they improve those raw spots between paving stones.

Just as a room feels unfinished without a floor cover, so even the most elegant garden (and certainly a slippery slope) seems incomplete without a ground cover. For a modest area rug, add ground-cover plants by the dozen. For a grand carpet, add them by the hundreds — and don't be afraid to mix and match contrasting species.

A slope-saving kaleidoscope includes a mixed and matched assortment of tough, ground-hugging perennials.

Plant spacing, as typically suggested on the label, is determined by the species' normal rate of growth. But since ground covers are often planted in staggered rows with lots of bare soil between, a new planting can look pretty awful. For this reason, I prefer to space them closely for an immediate effect and thin later if needed.

Ultimately, though, spacing decisions depend on the expanse to be covered and the available funds — not necessarily in that order.

COVERS THAT SPREAD STEADILY BUT NOT SO QUICKLY

Although plants chosen for ground covers are those that naturally enjoy spreading or flopping, some widen their circle at only a modest speed. The following move steadily but not especially quickly.

■ *Ajuga reptans* / **Ajuga or Bugleweed**

Hardy perennial

Zone 3

Sun and part or full shade

Imagine tiny romaine lettuces in a beautiful range of colors and you have a picture of the ajugas. Evergreen where winters are mild, ajugas can look bedraggled by March. But all is quickly forgiven once the small purple-blue or white spring flower spikes appear. If the area to be covered is large, experiment with adjacent swirls of hybrids with contrasting leaves such as 'Bronze Beauty' (deep crimson), 'Metallica Crispa' (silvery ruffled foliage), or 'Burgundy Glow' (a rich crimson, pink, and cream).

■ *Astilbe chinensis* 'Pumila' / **Chinese Astilbe**

Hardy perennial

Zone 5

Sun and part or full shade

All astilbes eventually spread. But for serious ground covering, 'Pumila' is the plant to use. Its finely cut leaves rarely exceed about 10 inches in height and eventually create a dense mat. In midsummer 8- to 10-inch-high fuzzy purple flower spikes rise above the foliage. All astilbes prefer moist soil, but this one will forgive should you forget to water.

Bugleweed (Ajuga reptans *'Burgundy Glow')* *is a steady spreader and bears its purple-blue flower spikes in spring.*

The bold leaves of bergenia (Bergenia cordifolia) *hold a slope along a steep stairway.*

A clump of variegated blue lilyturf (Liriope muscari) *brandishes its late-summer purple blooms.*

■ *Bergenia cordifolia* / **Bergenia** *(See photo on page 69.)*
Hardy perennial
Zone 3
Sun or light shade
When I hear talk of "bold" foliage, I think of bergenias with their foot-long, paddle-shaped leaves. Early spring brings tall pink flowers, while autumn turns the foliage a purple-bronze. Ideal conditions are rich soil and good moisture. Among the many hybrids are the large-leaved 'Margery Fish', which has pink flowers, and 'Silver Light', whose blooms are white.

■ *Juniperus horizontalis* / **Creeping Juniper** *(See photo on page 114.)*
Evergreen shrub
Zone 3
Sun or light shade
The many variations of this prostrate shrub with its long spreading or creeping branches are decorative ground covers all year long. The scaly needles of the aptly

named 'Blue Rug' juniper (*J. h.* 'Wiltonii') are indeed a silvery blue-green. Several cultivars, including those of 'Bar Harbor', turn a purple-bronze in winter.

■ *Liriope* spp. / Lilyturf and *Ophiopogon* spp. / Mondo Grass
Hardy perennials
Zones vary
Sun and part or full shade
At first glance, it's hard to tell the difference between these two ornamental grasses, but it doesn't matter, since both are terrific. Blue lilyturf *(L. muscari)* has leaves that grow to at least a foot and purple-blue to white summer flower spikes that are followed by tiny black berries. It is hardy to around Zone 6. An especially cheerful cultivar is *L. m.* 'Variegata', whose foliage is striped a creamy yellow. The moody-looking black mondo grass *Ophiopogon planiscapus* 'Nigrescens' (sometimes *O. p.* 'Arabicus') has deep maroon leaves that remain well under a foot. Its flower spikes are also shorter and followed by blue fruit. It is hardy to around Zone 7. If winter takes a toll on these normally evergreen grasses, shear them back in spring.

■ *Stachys byzantina* / **Lamb's-Ears** *(See photo on page 54.)*
Hardy perennial
Zone 4
Sun
Few can resist stopping to stroke these soft, furry leaves, which look (to this New Yorker, at least) more like a rabbit's ear than a lamb's. The handsome silvery green foliage and the fleshy stems are at their best in full sun and well-drained soil. Unfortunately, hot, humid days — and too many hosings — can reduce this plant to mush. For reasons I've never understood, some gardeners cut off the furry purple flower stalks. I think they're just dandy.

ADDITIONAL SLOW BUT STEADY GROUND COVERS

■ *Asarum* spp. / Wild Ginger
See page 18.

■ *Cotoneaster horizontalis* / **Rock Cotoneaster** *(See photo on page 48.)*
Evergreen or semievergreen shrub
Zone 5
Sun and part or full shade
This ground-hugging shrub with small leaves and bright autumn berries is best known for the herringbone pattern of its branches.

■ *Epimedium* **spp. / Epimedium**
See page 18.

■ *Hakonechloa macra* 'Aureola' / **Hakonechloa**
Hardy perennial
Zone 5
Part or light shade
This truly stunning yellow and green grass reaches about 8 inches in height and adds a delightful contrast in both texture and color.

> **TIPS FOR SUCCESS**
>
> **COPING WITH BULB LEAVES**
>
> Resist the temptation to neaten the leaves of spring bulbs by braiding or tying them. This decreases the leaf surface exposed to sunlight and inhibits the formation of the bud for next year's flower. Experiments by the Royal Horticultural Society have shown that after the flowers are gone, only six weeks is needed for the leaves to do their job. After that you can snip to your heart's content.

■ *Polygonatum* **spp. / Solomon's-seal** *(See photo on page 23.)*
Hardy perennial
Zones vary
Part or full shade
The various species of Solomon's-seals range from 1 to 6 feet in height. Variegated forms spread somewhat more slowly than the green ones.

■ *Tiarella cordifolia* / **Foamflower**
See page 24.

COVERS THAT SPREAD QUICKLY

The following ground covers spread rather quickly, and some can be quite invasive. These are good for quickly covering large areas or for areas where less-intrepid species falter.

Phlox means "flame" and well describes a field ignited by its ground cover of Phlox divaricata *and* P. subulata.

■ *Aegopodium podagraria* 'Variegatum' / Goutweed or Bishop's Weed

Hardy perennial

Zone 3

Sun and part or full shade

At first blush, these white-edged, delicate-looking leaves seem the ideal solution to areas in need of a tough cover. And that is definitely useful. But the obstinate quality that enables it to boldly grow where nothing else will makes it a real pest everywhere else. Forewarned is forearmed. A plus are the lacy white flowers in early summer.

■ *Cerastium tomentosum* / Snow-in-summer

Hardy perennial

Zone 3

Sun

A dense mat of this silvery ground cover will crowd out weeds in no time. But in return, it demands full sun and perfect drainage. True to its name, a veritable blizzard of white flowers obscures its narrow leaves in late spring and early summer. The hybrid 'Yo-Yo' flowers most freely but spreads less quickly.

■ *Ceratostigma plumbaginoides* / Plumbago or Leadwort

Hardy perennial

Zone 5

Sun or light shade

Because it's so slow to awaken in spring, my plumbago scares me each year into thinking it's disappeared. That would be a shame since I would sorely miss its cloud of late-summer purple-blue flowers and bronze autumn leaves. Moving unfettered along a low edging wall, it's never so rampant that it can't be kept in bounds.

■ *Houttuynia cordata* 'Chamaelon' / Chameleon Plant

Hardy perennial

Zone 3

Sun and part or full shade

A hint of blush splashes through the variegated green and cream tones giving these heart-shaped leaves a most cheerful face. This plant may quickly overtake anything in its wake, but this can be useful where dense shade and bare soil need brightening. Sun and lack of moisture will inhibit the rampage.

■ *Hypericum calycinum* / St.-John's-wort

Hardy perennial

Zone 5

Sun and part or full shade

The first time I saw this vigorous grower (also known as Aaron's Beard) I was charmed by its blanket of small golden yellow summer flowers. These crowned a dense cover of dark leaves, which can be evergreen or nearly so, depending on winter's severity. No problem if you forget to water.

> **TIPS FOR SUCCESS**
>
> **CHANGING pH**
>
> To make your soil more alkaline (which means raising the pH), add wood ashes, pulverized seashells, or eggshells. For a faster reaction, use ground horticultural limestone or dolomitic limestone. To make your soil more acid (lower the pH), add tea leaves, coffee grounds, or cottonseed meal. For a faster reaction, use aluminum sulfate, following package directions for quantity.

■ *Mentha spicata* / Spearmint

Hardy perennial

Zone 4

Sun or part shade

Spearmint is famous not only for its delightful fragrance, but for its joy in rambling rapidly through the garden. Use it as a ground cover and there'll be plenty of tasty leaves for drinks and stews. The small white or pale pink spiky flowers are a refreshing edible garnish.

■ *Potentilla tabernaemontani* also known as *P. verna* / Spring Cinquefoil

Hardy perennial

Zone 4

Sun or light shade

Buttery yellow spring flowers make this creeper a cheerful addition wherever its wandering stems take it. Although it grows to a height of just a few inches, my plants penetrate the tiniest cracks in a low rock wall. These are stalwart plants that spread quickly to form a solid cover with minimal care. *P. fruticosa* is a shrubbier cover that grows to about 2 feet.

Additional Fast-Growing Ground Covers

- *Adiantum pedatum* / Maidenhair Fern

Hardy perennial

Zone 4

Part or full shade

This charming plant with leaves arranged in a fan-shaped pattern spreads steadily but must have continually moist soil.

- *Galium odoratum* also sometimes *Asperula odorata* / Sweet Woodruff

Hardy perennial

Zone 5

Part sun or shade

This tidy-looking plant, with its small slender leaves arranged like the spokes of a wheel, has white flowers in spring.

- *Hedera helix* / English Ivy

Hardy evergreen vine

Zones vary

Sun and part or full shade

This tough vine will cheerfully scramble across the soil and climb walls.

- *Lamium maculatum* and *Lamiastrum galeobdolon* / Dead Nettle

Hardy perennials

Zone 3

Sun and part or full shade

These are two similar-looking plants: *Lamiastrum* has bright yellow spring flowers; *Lamium*'s are white or pink. Also look for the variegated-leaf cultivars.

- *Pachysandra terminalis* / Pachysandra or Japanese Spurge

Hardy evergreen perennial

Zone 4

Sun and part or full shade

If you're bored with this useful but overused plant, try patches of *P. t.* 'Variegata', whose leaves are splashed with white (although it's not as hardy as the species).

- *Viola* spp. / Violets

Hardy perennial
Zones vary
Sun and part or full shade
The rounded leaves of this old-fashioned favorite contrast nicely with other ground covers. Spring brings charming white or purple blooms.

CRACK FILLERS

Steady-growing, mat-type creepers help solve the problem of loose soil or weeds in the cracks between paving stones. The following are happy in tiny spaces and won't mind an occasional foot on their foliage.

- *Arenaria verna* / Irish Moss or Sandwort

Hardy perennial
Zone 3
Sun or part shade
This mossy-looking plant forms clumps of flat leaves. Its tiny flowers open in June.

- *Chamaemelum nobile* / Chamomile

Hardy perennial
Zone 4
Sun
The same fragrant leaves and small yellow flowers used in herbal teas have an equally intoxicating scent when stepped on.

- *Dianthus deltoides* / Maiden Pinks

Hardy perennial
Zone 3
Sun or light shade
In early summer the low mounds of maiden pinks have small pale pink or purple flowers. 'Albus' is white, 'Brilliant' is bright crimson.

Creeping mother-of-thyme (Thymus serpyllum) *won't mind an occasional foot on its intensely fragrant foliage.*

■ *Gypsophila repens* / Creeping Baby's-breath
Hardy perennial
Zone 4
Sun
The pale blue-green foliage and narrow leaves of this charmer are less than 6 inches high, and the white or pink flowers appear in summer.

■ *Mentha requienii* / Corsican Mint
Marginally hardy perennial
Zone 7
Sun or part shade
Tiny round leaves and thin rooting stems make this aromatic mint a real charmer and well worth replacing when harsh winters take a toll. Lilac-hued summer flowers appear on plants grown in the sun.

■ *Sedum anglicum* / **English Stonecrop**

Hardy evergreen perennial

Zone 4

Sun or light shade

Tiny fleshy leaves and tiny flowers form a dense 2-inch-high carpet on this tough species.

■ *Thymus* **spp.** / **Thyme** *(See photo on page 78.)*

Perennial

Zones vary

Sun

The thymes include several hundred deliciously fragrant, small-leaved creepers. Some are evergreen or nearly so. Common thyme *(T. vulgaris),* a culinary favorite since Colonial days, includes hybrids with variegated or lemon-scented leaves. Mother-of-thyme *(T. serpyllum)* eventually forms a dense mat with rose-purple early-summer flowers.

■ *Veronica repens* / **Creeping Speedwell**

Hardy perennial

Zone 5

Sun

In early summer, the tiny shiny leaves of this creeper disappear beneath a haze of small blue flowers. Look for white and pink hybrids.

Chapter 7:
Quick Fillers for Curbsides and Other Empty Spaces

If nature abhors a vacuum, gardeners abhor empty space. Certainly it's wise to heed the words of nurserymen who warn against crowding the garden. Plants do need air circulation as well as room to expand. But there's nothing as disheartening as staring at toothless gaps all summer while new shrubs or slow-growing perennials mature.

Some gardeners may opt to plant their new additions closely and move them apart after a few years. But I prefer to plug those unsightly holes immediately — if temporarily — by using quick-growing annuals and tender perennials. Although some of these plants are easily grown from seed, my goal is speed, so I use trays of nursery-grown seedlings. These transplants are not only faster, they're fail-safe.

Here are some quick-growing annuals and tender perennials to add height, bulk, or color to every empty summer space.

A luminous mix of cosmos and zinnias has an ageratum border.

Sidewalk Gardening

An empty space that's especially challenging — some say especially depressing — is the strip along the curb or beneath a street tree. This is a spot that pleads for planting with quick fillers for summer cheer.

But be warned: it's the height of masochism to plant here. Problems include soil so compacted it could be mistaken for concrete, lack of nutrients or organic matter, insufficient water through the summer heat, and an occasional disappearing plant. The greatest outrage, though, may be having this meager parcel used as an outhouse for dogs (few dog owners realize these visits eventually kill trees and flowers).

Colorful ti plants (Cordyline terminalis) *are well suited to a sidewalk site with heat, high humidity, and light shade.*

Sidewalk gardening isn't easy. But I believe it's worth the effort it takes to improve the street scene and the neighborhood. And as far as I know, no city has posted any rules or regs against this. On the contrary, most municipalities are thrilled when citizens care enough to do their planting in public.

The first rule of curbside gardening is to be generous, especially near areas of heavy pedestrian use. Start with good-sized, bushy plants, preferably already in flower, and place them close together. For reasons no scientist has chosen to probe, walkers (and dog owners) rarely promenade through a dense mass of colorful blooms.

The second rule is to use practical plants. A busy curb is no place to show off your expertise with rare or exotic species. Choose instead those

that can survive when you're away, can withstand an occasional misplaced foot, appear minimally inspiring to thieves, and will not be expensive to replace.

Short annuals and tender perennials are best used in the immediate area around street trees since their roots are minimal competition for nutrients and water. Hardy perennials are better where root space is more ample. Shallow perennial ground covers are useful too (see chapter 6) especially when combined with colorful summer flowers.

Before planting, loosen and improve the soil and add compost or leaf mold and several trowels of an all-purpose granular fertilizer. Once the plants are in place, continued maintenance is essential: regular watering, of course, but just as important is cleaning away papers and debris and replacing damaged or missing plants quickly.

■ *Abutilon hybridum* / **Flowering Maple also known as Chinese Bell Flower**

Sun or part shade

Yellow, white, pink, or red bell-shaped flowers cover these tropical shrubs that grow over 4 feet tall. Some have leaves variegated green and gold.

■ *Ageratum houstonianum* / **Ageratum** *(See photo on page 80.)*

Sun or part shade

These purple-blue flowers remind me of fluffy little pincushions. Heights of the many hybrids vary from 6 inches to over 2 feet.

■ *Amaranthus caudatus* / **Love-lies-bleeding**

Sun

It's hard to resist a plant with a name like this. Strange fuzzy ropes of tiny bright red flowers up to 2 feet long appear on these 4-foot-high plants. Dry them for winter arrangements.

> **TIPS FOR SUCCESS**
>
> **POT-BOUND PLANTS**
>
> Plants are not too smart. If your new nursery acquisition has a tightly wrapped mass of roots, scratch and loosen the surface before transplanting into your garden. If you don't, the roots will continue to grow in an ever-tighter ball, and the plant will die.

■ *Begonia semperflorens* / **Begonia**

Sun or part shade

A nearly nonstop bloomer from the tropics, begonias have flowers in pink, white, and red, and leaves in green and red. In cold climates, take them indoors for continued bloom and winter color. Grows to a bushy 12 inches.

■ *Browallia americana* or *B. elata* / **Browallia**

Sun or part shade

The purple-blue somewhat bell-shaped flowers of browallia grow on bushy, floppy 2-foot stems. A cousin of the petunia, it is also good as a summer ground cover and in hanging baskets.

■ *Caladium bicolor* / **Caladium**

Part shade or shade

This tropical tuber produces its large, delicate-looking heart-shaped leaves on skinny 1- to 2-foot high stems. Colors are patterns of red, pink, green, and white.

Where space permits, sunflowers are an irresistible curbside trim.

■ *Canna generalis* / Canna

Sun

Flowers in bright reds, oranges, or yellows splashed with contrasting spots and dots nestle neatly among huge paddle-shaped leaves. Heights vary from 2 to 8 feet, with leaves toned with green, red, and now also gold stripes.

■ *Celosia* spp. / Celosia or Cockscomb

Sun

Strange velvety-crested or -plumed flowers in vibrant reds, yellows, oranges, and purples top these 1- to 4-foot plants. Save the flowers for use in dried arrangements.

■ *Cleome spinosa* or *C. hassleriana* / Spiderflower

Sun or light shade

Pink, purple, or white spidery-looking flowers top 4-foot-tall stems on this native tropical American.

- *Cosmos bipinnatus* / Cosmos

Sun

Wispy-looking 3-foot-tall foliage is dotted through summer with elegant cup-shaped blooms in shades of pink, white, carmine, and yellow gold. Cut the flowers freely for fresh bouquets.

- *Gomphrena globosa* / Globe Amaranth

Sun or light shade

Small round flowers in white, purple, pink, or orange top bushy 1- to 2-foot-tall plants. The little globes are delightful in fresh bouquets, and I dry them for use later on my Christmas tree and in the winter window box.

- *Helianthus annuus* / Sunflower

Sun

These glorious sun-shaped flowers are typically a golden yellow and now also red, purplish, and bicolor blends. The sturdy stems grow to 4 feet and higher.

- *Hypoestes phyllostachya* / Polka-dot Plant

See page 31.

- *Impatiens wallerana* / Impatiens

See page 21.

- *Lantana camara* / Lantana

See page 49.

The reliable, easily grown impatiens are a distinct favorite for use in challenging sidewalk locations.

- *Lavatera trimestris* / Mallow also Rose Mallow

Sun or light shade

Hibiscus-like flowers in pink or white cover this 3-foot-tall annual that looks for all the world like a shrub. Native to the Mediterranean, its huge mid- to late-summer flowers benefit from regular deadheading.

Cut and Dry

Cut and then dry summer flowers such as globe amaranth, cockscomb, or yarrow, and save them for use in winter arrangements. Do your cutting in early morning, just as the blossoms reach their peak, and gather the stems with a rubber band. Dry them in a well-ventilated spot, away from the sun, and upside down (hydrangeas prefer to be right side up). They'll be dry within two days to two weeks depending on the humidity, temperature, and species.

- *Mirabilis jalapa* / **Four-o'clock**

Sun or light shade

As the name implies, these nearly 3-foot-tall plants do their thing in the late afternoon. The profusion of white, red, or sometimes yellow funnel-shaped flowers invariably self-sow with abandon.

- *Ocimum basilicum* / **Basil**

Sun or light shade

This is a delicious filler whose use lies more in its lush leaves than its slender pale lavender blooms. The various tasty hybrids have foliage in many sizes and scents, including several with handsome purple foliage that needs full sun. Heights vary to about 15 inches.

- *Pelargonium hortorum* / **Geranium**

Sun or part shade

This classic flower of window box fame has white, pink, salmon, and red blooms and can grow well over 2 feet. A few of the many hybrids also have variegated leaves.

- *Pennisetum setaceum* / **Purple or Crimson Fountain Grass**

Sun or light shade

This tender perennial grass is a stunning summer filler with its bronze narrow leaves and rose-colored or purple feathery plumes. The 4-foot-high stems are superb for fresh as well as dried arrangements.

Lavender-hued petunias and ageratum enhance the top of a rock wall.

- *Petunia hybrida* / Petunia

Sun or light shade

It's hard to imagine summer without petunias, which now flower in nearly every color and include double forms and stripes. This floppy plant can vary in length from 1 to 2½ feet and is also a good summer ground cover or container or hanging-basket cascade.

- *Ricinus communis* / Castor Bean

Sun

These 6- to 8-foot-tall plants, with oversized leaves and small red or creamy yellow flowers are real garden showstoppers. Beware the decorative seedpods, which are poisonous if eaten.

A luxuriant blend of white petunias, yellow marigolds, and pale purple lantana has a trailer of variegated vinca.

- *Salpiglossis sinuata* / Painted Tongue

Sun

These large funnel-shaped flowers are carmine, violet-pink, or gold with unusual contrasting veins colored yellow, maroon, or blue. A trailing plant that grows to about 3 feet, it is also a good summer ground cover.

- *Salvia splendens* / Salvia

Sun or part shade

Vibrant flower spikes in red, pink, cream, or purple-blues extend the height of this plant to about 24 inches. The flowers are excellent in either fresh or dried arrangements.

- *Senecio cineraria* / Dusty Miller

See page 47.

Winter's Price

The toll exacted by deicing compounds on sidewalks, driveways, and roadsides is apparent by summer in the form of dead or dying shrubs and trees. The best way to counter this soil toxicity is to add gypsum (the common name of hydrated calcium sulfate). Work it into the soil at the rate of about 10 pounds for each 250 square feet in soil of affected area.

- *Tagetes* spp. / **Marigold**   *(See photo on page 88.)*

Sun or light shade

The versatile, pungent-scented marigolds produce creamy white to yellow and deep orange flowers in many shapes and sizes. Height varies from 8 to 24 inches.

- *Torenia fournieri* / **Wishbone Flower**

Sun or part shade

These tiny orchidlike flowers from tropical Asia have blue, pink, white, and plum colored blooms on bushy 10-inch stems. Keep them well watered for good repeat bloom.

- *Tropaeolum majus* / **Nasturtium**

Sun or light shade

These floppy flowers make good summer ground covers or container and hanging-basket edgers, and the edible blooms are a pungent garnish on summer salads. Colors include yellow, orange, crimson, salmon, and pink, some with variegated green-and-white leaves. Height varies from 6 inches to about 3 feet.

They may not speed the mail, but a surrounding of Sedum spectabile *should make the mailman smile.*

Chapter 8:

Late-Season Bloomers for Late-Season Blues

Sometime around the middle of August I find myself wishing for winter. Those giddy hues that dazzle spring are now but a memory, and summer's heat and pests are definitely taking a toll. Corners of the garden are looking a tad tired, and I renew my vow, yet again, to save my time, energy, and space for species that give maximum pleasure.

If by now a plant has proven less than successful or has repeatedly yielded to insects or disease, then it's time for a change. Give it away or throw it away, but get it out of the garden. As the legendary mistress of Sissinghurst in England, Vita Sackville-West, once said, "If it displeases you the first year, get rid of it, for it will succeed in displeasing you every year thereafter." For sure!

But then what? By happy coincidence, high summer is also high bargain time at nurseries, so it is often possible to save some money while filling those wretched holes. Those in the know also spend late-season weekends scouring nurseries for plants that shine as autumn makes its entrance. Many of these ornamental shrubs, perennials, and even a few annuals, are handsome from late summer well into fall.

A purple splash of asters vies for attention with the crimson autumn leaves of a sourwood tree (Oxydendron arboreum) *and the fuzzy blooms of sedum 'Autumn Joy'.*

Here is a selection of late-season bloomers to alleviate those late-season blues — and add another spell of glory to the garden.

LATE-SEASON PERENNIALS AND ANNUALS

- *Anemone* spp. / Japanese Anemone

Perennial

Zone 6

Sun or part shade

I can't imagine facing summer's end without the carefree, long-blooming Japanese anemones (many of which come from China as well as England and Germany). The dainty 1- to 2-inch saucer-shaped flowers seem to dance atop the 2- to 4-foot-high stems all autumn. Although botanical names include *A. hupehensis japonica, A. vitifolia,* and *A. hybrida,* most are simply known by their hybrid names, among them the white-flowered 'Alba' and the various pink flowers of 'Robustissima', 'Prince Henry', and 'September Charm' (which says it all).

- *Aster* spp. / Aster or Michaelmas Daisy

Hardy perennial

Zones vary

Sun

The asters are a large, mostly confusing group that includes many easily grown late-summer bloomers that self-sow with abandon. Notables include the New England aster *(A. novae-angliae),* a wildflower whose inch-wide blooms are typically purple although pink shades are found on 'Alma Potschke' and 'Harrington's Pink'. *A. frikartii,* developed in Switzerland after World War I, has fragrant, 3-inch-wide lavender-blue flowers on 2½-foot stems. 'Wonder of Staffa' is an exceptionally long bloomer.

- *Capsicum* spp. / Peppers

Tender perennial

Sun or light shade

Fall harvest means pumpkins to some, but peppers to me. Like lettuce, young

The easily grown Japanese anemones (Anemone hybrida) *flower freely and need no staking.*

Late summer means dazzling bouquets of asters.

Black-eyed Susan (Rudbeckia nitida) *and butterfly bush* (Buddleia davidii) *welcome the end of summer.*

ornamental pepper plants are among the late-summer offerings found at many nurseries. These diminutive plants have decorative red, yellow, or purple fruit that last well into autumn. The white and yellow flowers continue to develop as long as the nights are frost-free. But take care. Many of these "hot" peppers really are. So don't lick your fingers after harvesting, and don't touch your eyes.

■ *Lactuca sativa* / **Lettuce**

Annual

Sun or part shade

Lettuce is a cool-weather crop, which means that lettuce seedlings are available in nurseries in late summer (as well as early spring). For handsome, edible fillers and edging plants, choose from among the numerous decorative shapes and the various red and green leaf tones and textures. Keep them well watered, and harvest your own salad greens for weeks by snipping two or three outer leaves at a time.

■ *Malva* spp. / Mallow

Perennial

Zones vary

Sun or light shade

The vigorous mallows bloom freely from midsummer through early autumn. The hollyhock mallow (*M. alcea* 'Fastigata') reaches about 4 feet and covers itself with many pale pink blooms. The musk mallow (*M. moschata* 'Alba') has white flowers on 2-foot-high stems and often self-sows new plants in welcome places.

■ *Perovskia atriplicifolia* / **Russian Sage**

Hardy perennial

Zone 5

Sun

The sage in the name here comes from the sagelike fragrance that the bruised leaves impart. Late summer brings a soft blue haze of 3- to 5-foot-tall flowers above lacy, silvery leaves. For strong stems and good blooms, cut the stalks to the ground in early spring. 'Filagran' has exceptionally fine filigree leaves.

■ *Phlox paniculata* / **Phlox or Garden Phlox** *(See photo on page 73.)*

Hardy perennial

Zone 3

Sun or light shade

The name "phlox" means flame, and that's a good description for this delightful group of easily grown plants that brighten the late-summer garden. Quickly reaching at least 3 feet, the stately stems bear long-lasting flowers in colors from red, pink, and purple to white. Thin the plants in early summer to increase air circulation and avoid unsightly mildews in autumn.

■ *Rudbeckia nitida* 'Herbstonne' / **Black-eyed Susan or Coneflower**

Perennial

Zone 4

Sun or part shade

The showstopper in my high-summer garden is this huge plant with its 4-inch-wide, sulfur yellow daisylike flowers. Although apt to droop after a drenching storm, the 5-foot-tall stems are worth every bit of staking time they take. The large green seedpods that develop from the high central cones linger to decorate the winter snow as fuzzy dark brown dots.

LATE-SEASON WOODY PLANTS

■ *Abelia grandiflora* / Abelia or Glossy Abelia
Semievergreen shrub
Zone 6
Sun or light shade
Although severe frosts will cut this shrub to the ground, the new season's growth quickly reaches 4 feet by midsummer. This is when the funnel-shaped flowers appear, strongly resembling their cousin, the honeysuckle. A hybrid of several Chinese species, the abelia is valued for its dense, low-growing branches. 'Edward Goucher' has deep pink flowers and can reach 5 feet.

■ *Buddleia davidii* / **Butterfly Bush or Summer Lilac** *(See photo on page 94.)*
Shrub
Zone 5
Sun or part shade
Even in my mid-Manhattan garden, butterflies find this aptly named fragrant shrub and linger, seemingly intoxicated, on its fragrant blossoms. To encourage repeat bloom, snip away the long narrow flowers as they fade; to encourage sturdy new growth, cut the stems to the ground in early spring. 'African Queen' and 'Black Knight' have stunning deep purple flowers, 'Snow Bank' has white, and 'Dubonnet' has deep red ones. 'Lochinch' has blue-lavender flowers and originated with the Earl of Stair Lochinch, Scotland.

TIPS FOR SUCCESS

EPSOM SALT

Epsom salt is not only a good balm for soothing aching human limbs — it's a good nutrient for plants, especially roses. Epsom salt (actually magnesium sulfate) promotes new stem growth and helps relieve one of the soil deficiencies that causes loss of leaf color (called chlorosis). Toss two handfuls around each shrub in spring and fall (and use what's left over in your bath after planting). Epsom salt is sold at drug stores.

■ *Clethra alnifolia* / Summersweet or Sweet Pepper Bush

Shrub

Zone 4

Sun or part shade

In whaling days, this intensely fragrant plant was called sailor's delight, very likely because those on returning ships picked up the scent before they saw land. The aromatic 4-inch-long fuzzy, white or pale pink blooms are followed by prominent brown seedpods that linger through winter if not clipped for use in a holiday wreath. The leaves are pale yellow in autumn. 'Rosea' has pale pink flowers.

> **TIPS FOR SUCCESS**
>
> **SPRING BULB ORDERS**
>
> It's easy to procrastinate on placing orders for tulips, daffodils, and other spring bloomers. But since these bulbs must be planted in fall, orders must be sent to suppliers before Labor Day to avoid shipping delays. Do your planning on a simple sketch of your garden, and do experiment with at least one new species each year.

■ *Hibiscus syriacus* / Rose-of-Sharon

Shrub

Zone 5

Sun or light shade

If you've been to the tropics, you'll recognize the fist-sized funnel-shaped flowers of the rose-of-Sharon. But this is the only truly hardy shrub in the genus. A favorite of the Victorians, this Chinese native can be trimmed to bush size or pruned to a single stem for a 10- to 15-foot tree. 'Diana' has large white flowers, 'Woodbridge' has rosy red flowers, 'Blushing Bride' has double pink blooms, and 'Bluebird' is pale blue with burgundy centers.

■ *Itea virginica* 'Henry's Garnet' / Virginia Sweetspire

Shrub

Zone 6

Sun or part and full shade

Woodland strollers in late summer stop in their tracks when they see the 8-inch-long creamy blossoms of this tough native plant. It cheerfully adapts to a wide range of growing conditions including moist, acid soils near streams. If left unchecked, this plant will eventually form a dense colony of slender 4- to 7-foot-tall stems. Autumn foliage is a glowing red-purple.

ADDITIONAL LATE-SEASON BLOOMERS

- *Begonia grandis* / Hardy Begonia

Hardy perennial

Zone 5

Light or full shade

This tough begonia, with tidy heart-shaped leaves, bears its cascading pink or white flowers from late summer to late autumn.

- *Boltonia asteroides* 'Snowbank' / Boltonia

Hardy perennial

Zone 4

Sun

The white asterlike flowers appear as a frothy topping on 4-foot stems.

- *Brassica oleracea acephala* / Ornamental Kale

Annual vegetable

Sun or part shade

This cabbage family member has large decorative foliage in tones of pink, white, and green. Wow the neighbors and add it to your fading late-season window box.

- *Caryopteris clandonensis* / Blue Spirea or Bluebeard

Shrub

Zone 5

Sun

This 2-foot-high shrub from Asia has beautiful powder blue fringed flowers.

- *Clematis maximowicziana* or sometimes *C. paniculata* / Sweet Autumn Clematis

Hardy deciduous vine

Zone 6

Sun or part shade

The clouds of fragrant white fluffy flowers that cover this vine in late summer are followed by equally fluffy seedpods that linger late into winter.

TIPS FOR SUCCESS

SAFE COMPOST

It's not a good idea to add diseased or insect-covered leaves to your compost pile. Disease spores and insect eggs are destroyed when compost reaches a very high temperature. But since the piles that most home gardeners tend are rarely large enough to attain such levels of heat, diseased leaves should be discarded with the trash.

Use branches of cut blooms of the peegee hydrangea (Hydrangea paniculata) *for long-lasting autumn arrangements indoors.*

■ *Hibiscus moscheutos* / Rose Mallow

Hardy perennial
Zone 5
Sun or light shade
This shrubby 3-foot-tall perennial has eye-catching hibiscus-like flowers in dinner-plate size, colored red, pink, and white.

■ *Hydrangea paniculata* 'Grandiflora' / Peegee Hydrangea

Deciduous shrub or small tree
Zone 6
Sun or part shade
The large conical clusters of white flowers can be dried for indoor arrangements or left in place to fade outside in winter.

The lavender-pink flowers of obedient plant (Physostegia virginiana) *are a showy display in the late-season garden.*

■ *Lobelia cardinalis* / Cardinal Flower *(See photo on page 33.)*
See page 37.

■ *Nipponanthemum nipponicum* or *Chrysanthemum nipponicum* / **Nippon or Montauk Daisy**
See page 47.

■ *Physostegia virginiana* / Obedient Plant or False Dragonhead
Hardy perennial
Zone 4
Sun or light shade
The peculiar, tubular, lipped pink flowers top nearly 2-foot-high stems. If moved, they will not spring back into position, but "obediently" remain in place.

- *Sedum spectabile* / **Stonecrop** *(See photo on page 89.)*

Hardy perennial
Zone 4
Sun or light shade
The species itself is outstanding, but also look for hybrids 'Autumn Joy', 'Brilliant', 'Ruby Glow', and 'Vera Jameson'.

- *Vitex agnus-castus* / **Chaste Tree** *(See photo on page 42.)*

See page 50.

The late-summer garden should be an exuberant mass of foliage and color.

CHAPTER 9:
PLANTS FOR CONTAINERS AND OTHER CLOSE QUARTERS

Fans of Louis XIV may argue that Versailles was the first container garden of note. But his 3,000 tubbed trees are a mere ho-hum compared to the plants we now jam into pots on our windowsills, balconies, terraces, doorsteps, and decks.

Most gardeners feel their space is limited. But when I think of small spaces, I think of landscapes measured in feet or even inches. This includes not only containers on a rooftop or penthouse (where I once did my gardening) and the tiny city yard (where I garden now), but those peculiar slivers of leftover land, like the strip my daughter now tends between her car and a fence.

Where space is limited, every inch counts, and I always jam in more plants than I've room for. This means planting in layers — which mostly means adding low species under the tall. Dusty miller and leadwort, for example, brighten the feet of roses. Basil and thyme are good for surrounding tomatoes. And ferns and hellebores nestle beneath the rhododendron.

But crowded conditions are no better for plants than for people. So making

A splendid display is possible with clusters of containers in various sizes, shapes, and materials.

the most of limited space also means girth control, that is, the pruning or cutting away of portions of plants that spread. In a small space it's really not practical to allow the rampant growth that nature prefers — so a well-sharpened pruner is essential.

Then, too, a rampant plant in a tub can be exhausting to try to contain. So where space is minimal, it's best to start with plants whose natural rate of development tends to be slow or whose ultimate size is limited.

Here's a sampling of some plants well suited to containers or other close quarters. (Also see the Espalier on page 12 and Covers That Spread Steadily but Not So Quickly on page 68.)

Container Size

When it comes to containers for summer flowers, anything goes — from expired automobile tires to antique urns, any receptacle that is weatherproof, nontoxic to plants, and has a bottom opening for drainage. But when it comes to containers for hardy species — cold-climate trees, shrubs, and perennials — the receptacle must be large enough to sustain life over the winter. The more soil between the roots and the cold, the greater the chance of winter survival. In New York City (the cusp of Zones 6 and 7), where I do my gardening, I've found that a practical, *minimum* dimension for containers for hardy plants is 14 inches — in width, height, and length. In colder zones, this minimum must be increased; in warmer climates, it can be reduced. But wherever possible, bigger is better since *maintenance chores are inversely proportional to container size.*

ANNUALS AND PERENNIALS FOR CLOSE QUARTERS

■ *Ageratum houstonianum* / Ageratum *(See photo on page 80.)*
See page 83.

■ *Antirrhinum majus* / Snapdragon
Tender perennial
Sun
The many varieties and hybrids of the common snapdragon bear their tiny florets along graceful spires. Colors vary from white and yellow to pink and purple, and heights range from the dwarfs of several inches to stately stems of over 2 feet.

Every inch counts in a doorside container planting of tomatoes, petunias, and coleus.

■ *Begonia semperflorens* / **Begonia**
See page 83.

■ *Caladium bicolor* / **Caladium**
See page 83.

■ *Corydalis lutea* / **Corydalis**
Hardy perennial
Zone 5
Sun and light or part shade
Carefree small yellow flowers cover the foot-high mounds of corydalis for much of the summer. This neat plant has handsome, ferny-looking blue-green leaves that resemble its cousins, the bleeding-hearts. If happy in your garden, it will self-sow easily in delightful spots where you'll probably let it stay.

■ *Dicentra eximia* / Fringed Bleeding-heart

Hardy perennial

Zone 4

Sun and light or part shade

These neat, foot-high drifts of fine-textured blue-gray foliage last until frost and produce blooms throughout the summer. Give it rich, somewhat moist soil and it will freely self-sow, but the unwanted seedlings are easily removed.

■ *Nicotiana alata* / Flowering Tobacco

Tender perennial

Sun or light shade

Even nonsmokers will love this blooming cousin of the crop grown for cigarettes. Its 1- to 3-foot-high stems bear gracefully drooping, trumpet-shaped blooms in red, pink, chartreuse, or white that appear sporadically all summer. With insufficient sun, the plants will flop and flowering will cease.

■ *Pelargonium hortorum* / Geranium

See page 86.

■ *Tagetes* spp. / Marigold *(See photo on page 88.)*

See page 89.

■ *Thymus* spp. / Thyme *(See photo on page 78.)*

See page 79.

■ *Tulipa* spp. / Tulips

Bulb

Zones vary

Sun or light shade

A seemingly infinite assortment of tulips are available for tucking into containers and other small spaces. Planted in autumn, these bulbs emerge several months later to brighten spring with colors that span the rainbow. Where planting space is limited, it's best to replace tulip bulbs yearly.

TIPS FOR SUCCESS

WHEN TO PRUNE

There's nothing so frustrating as waiting for a shrub or tree to flower only to discover that in your zeal to prune, you've cut off the buds. The easiest way to avoid this blooper is to trim flowering plants immediately after they bloom.

WOODY PLANTS FOR CLOSE QUARTERS

- *Abelia grandiflora* / Abelia or Glossy Abelia

Hardy semievergreen shrub

Zone 6

Sun or light shade

Left uncut, the abelias can reach at least 6 feet, but hard shearing is acceptable for girth control. Even better for small spaces are 'Francis Mason', a variegated dwarf with foliage variegated green and yellow, and 'Prostrata', which rarely tops 2 feet.

- *Acer palmatum* cultivars / Japanese Maple

Hardy deciduous shrub or small tree

Zones vary

Sun and light or part shade

The seemingly infinite cultivars of Japanese maple are notable for their delicate red foliage and exotically layered limbs. Most hues fade by midsummer but color again in fall. If left untrimmed, these plants eventually develop a large and rounded outline. Some are slow growers but many are not, so look for those marked "dwarf" and control with regular pruning.

> **TIPS FOR SUCCESS**
>
> **REUSING CONTAINER SOIL**
>
> Save your container and window box soils for reuse each year. In early spring, before planting, increase its fertility and improve its friability by stirring in a blend of equal amounts of perlite, and compost, or cow manure. Just before planting, mix in several handfuls of a 5-10-5 granular fertilizer.

- *Daphne burkwoodii* 'Carol Mackie' / Daphne 'Carol Mackie'

Hardy semievergreen shrub

Zone 4

Sun or part shade

This truly delightful slow-growing shrub has a somewhat mounded form and rarely tops 3 to 4 feet in height and width. Its gold- or cream-edged leaves are always neat and handsome. Spring brings a profusion of starry pale pink flowers whose fragrance is intoxicating.

Only a few feet are needed to create a luxuriant dooryard planting of shrubs, perennials, and grasses.

■ *Ilex crenata* 'Compacta' / Dwarf Japanese Holly
Hardy broad-leaved evergreen
Zone 6
Sun and light or part shade
These compact plants typically grow to around 4 feet. But since they take well to shearing, I keep mine trimmed to under 3 feet. The small, glossy, dark green leaves densely cover its many tiny branches.

■ *Juniperus squamata* 'Blue Star' / Blue Star Juniper
Hardy needle evergreen shrub
Zone 4
Sun or light shade
Dense clusters of silvery blue needles cover this slow grower that can take years to reach its 2 feet of width and height. Full sun is typically recommended, but this plant added a colorful, foot-high mound for years in my partly shaded yard.

Snug in their small containers, parsley, patio tomatoes, and nasturtium await their turn in the salad bowl.

■ *Microbiota decussata* / Microbiota or Russian Arborvitae

Hardy evergreen shrub

Zone 2

Sun and part shade

This tough little evergreen was discovered in Siberia in the early 1900s. Although rarely taller than a foot, its width invariably exceeds its height, and the lacy cedar-like foliage makes an unusual ground cover. The winter sun turns the normally bright green hue a rusty-purple.

■ *Pinus mugo* / Dwarf Mugo Pine or Dwarf Swiss Mountain Pine

Hardy needle evergreen

Zone 4

Sun or light shade

As its name implies, this bushy dwarf does indeed grow in Switzerland. And while rarely rising above 4 feet, it can eventually spread to twice that width. Within the species there is tremendous variation, and nursery labels are rarely to be trusted. You'll know your plant was mislabeled when its gets to be bigger than you are. A yearly spring pruning will keep it in bounds.

■ *Pinus nigra* 'Globosa' / **Dwarf Austrian Pine**
Evergreen tree
Zone 4
Sun
This slow-growing evergreen is a dwarf form of the Austrian pine. Like the larger plant, it has stiff needles that are a shiny dark green that should serve well as a foil for softly colored annuals or perennials.

■ *Rhododendron* **spp. / Rhododendron and Azalea** *(See photo on page 27.)*
See page 26.

■ *Rosa* **spp. / Rose**
Hardy deciduous shrub
Zones vary
Sun and light shade
Roses are truly versatile plants and certainly at home in a container or other small space. The many classifications are not readily defined, but popular shrub forms include the floribundas (bushy plants with clusters of flowers), the hybrid teas (taller plants with one flower to a stem), and the miniatures or minis (diminutive bushes usually under 2 feet with flowers smaller than a quarter). The Flower Carpet roses, now widely seen at garden centers, resemble the floribundas and flower freely all season.

■ *Vaccinium corymbosum* / **Blueberry or Highbush Blueberry**
Hardy deciduous shrub
Zone 4
Sun or light shade
Yes, you can grow blueberries even if your garden is postage-stamp size. Blueberries are incomparable for multiseasonal interest (cream-colored flowers in summer and crimson autumn leaves) as well as for sublime edible fruit. You'll need

Some gardeners enjoy jamming in more plants than they seem to have room for.

rich, somewhat acid soil, and two plants with overlapping bloom sequences to ensure pollination. Cultivars — in order of flower appearance — include 'Earliblue', 'Patriot', 'Blueray', 'Bluecrop', 'Berkeley', 'Herbert', and 'Coville'. My two plants occupied a single 24-inch-wide tub for years and yielded countless pints of delicious fruit.

■ *Viburnum carlesii* 'Compactum' / Korean Spice Viburnum
Hardy deciduous shrub
Zone 5
Sun or light shade
With hundreds of species of viburnum, there's one for every spot. 'Compactum' is the shorter version of this densely rounded species whose stiff limbs can reach to about 6 feet. The white intensely fragrant snowball-shaped blooms emerge in spring from glossy red-hued buds.

DOWN MAY BE BETTER THAN UP: WEEPING TREES

Weeping plants — those whose limbs grow down, not up — are spectacular sculptures in winter and graceful accents in summer. Their limited vertical growth makes the weeping trees especially practical for a tiered balcony or an awning-covered patio where ceiling height is restricted.

Unfortunately, when pendulous species are considered, it's the weeping willow that springs to mind. But this is a quick-growing tree that soon grabs more than its fair share of room. It is not at all useful for a small space or container and I would never recommend it.

The weepers to purchase, instead, are the slow growers, whose ultimate height may be 2 to 15 feet.

■ *Cedrus atlantica* 'Glauca Pendula' / Weeping Blue Atlas Cedar
Hardy needle evergreen tree
Zone 6
Sun or light shade
This exotic-looking evergreen bears its clusters of silvery blue needles along sinewy, flexible limbs. Allow the drooping boughs to trail outward as they naturally grow, loop them around in a corkscrew or spiral, or stretch them horizontally so the hanging branchlets form a wispy curtain.

■ *Malus* spp. / Weeping Crab Apple
Hardy deciduous tree
Zones vary
Sun or light shade
Crab apple species and cultivars number in the hundreds, and pendulous forms abound. Flower colors range from white to pale pink and deep crimson. Rampant crossbreeding and inaccurate labeling mean you may never know your plant's name, but you'll get the color you want if you purchase when it's in bloom. Small red or orange edible fruit in late summer is followed by golden-red fall foliage. An old favorite, 'Red Jade', developed in 1933 by the Brooklyn Botanic Garden, has pale pink flowers and brilliant red berries. Prune crab apples immediately after flowering if needed for height and width control.

■ *Prunus* spp. / Weeping Cherry

Hardy deciduous tree

Zones vary

Sun

Pendulous branches and pale pink or white flowers distinguish the many spectacular weeping cherries. The weeping Higan cherry has pale pink blooms, and 'White Fountain' is true to its name. If pruning is needed, do so after it flowers.

■ *Pyrus salicifolia* 'Silver Frost' / **Weeping Willowleaf Pear**

Hardy deciduous tree

Zone 5

Sun

It was in England that I first fell for this stunning silvery gray tree whose narrow leaves resemble those of the weeping willow. A cascade of delicate white flowers covers the pendulous limbs in spring. Although it rarely exceeds 12 feet in height, it can spread considerably.

■ *Ulmus glabra* 'Camperdownii' / **Weeping Camperdown Elm**

Hardy deciduous tree

Zone 5

Sun and light shade

No need to fear the dread Dutch elm disease with this species. Just rejoice in the arching limbs that spread outward and trail gracefully. For years, this tough plant graced a container on my rooftop, impervious to wind or ice.

Topiary Whimsies

Gardeners love messing with Mother Nature. And the topiary, a plant sheared into a fanciful shape, is an excellent accent or focal point. Adding topiary is like adding sculpture. Pair two to flank a formal entry, or line several in a row to define a path or edge a stair.

The name originated in ancient Rome where elaborate ornamental gardens, or *topia*, were tended by slaves known as *topiari*. A seemingly limitless range of outlines have since evolved and for a reasonable sum, you can buy topiary triangles, cubes, spirals, spheres, tiered globes, and even small animals and birds.

Hardy species for topiaries include juniper, azalea, box, privet, and euonymus. Tender plants include rosemary, myrtle, scented geranium, flowering maple, camellia, and lantana.

Hardiness Zone Map

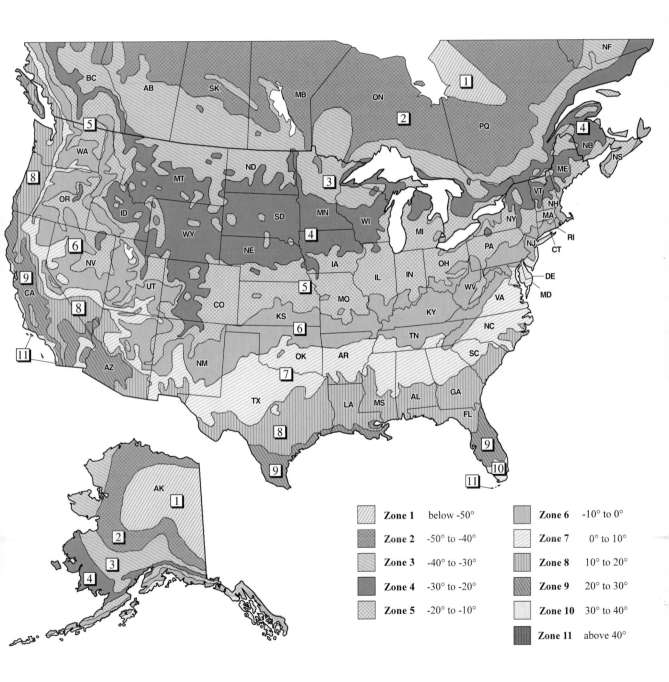

	Zone 1	below -50°	Zone 6	-10° to 0°
	Zone 2	-50° to -40°	Zone 7	0° to 10°
	Zone 3	-40° to -30°	Zone 8	10° to 20°
	Zone 4	-30° to -20°	Zone 9	20° to 30°
	Zone 5	-20° to -10°	Zone 10	30° to 40°
			Zone 11	above 40°

PHOTO CREDITS

Karen Bussolini: vi–1, 2, 12, 19, 21, 22, 30, 36, 38, 45, 46, 48, 50, 57, 59, 90, 101, 102, 109, 114

Ken Druse: 15, 16, 23, 32, 34, 35, 41, 42, 51, 53, 54, 56, 60, 66, 69 top, 73, 80, 93 top, bottom, 99, 100

Linda Yang: 7, 10, 14, 27, 29, 52, 62, 69 bottom, 70, 78, 82, 84, 85, 87, 88, 89, 94, 105, 108, 111, back cover

INDEX

Page numbers in italics refer to illustrations.

Titles available in the Taylor's Weekend Gardening Guides series:

Organic Pest and Disease Control	$12.95
Safe and Easy Lawn Care	12.95
Window Boxes	12.95
Attracting Birds and Butterflies	12.95
Water Gardens	12.95
Easy, Practical Pruning	12.95
The Winter Garden	12.95
Backyard Building Projects	12.95
Indoor Gardens	12.95
Plants for Problem Places	12.95

At your bookstore or by calling 1-800-225-3362

Prices subject to change without notice